Upper Playground 10 Years of T-Shirt Graphics
First Published in the United States of America,
by Gingko Press
In association with Upper Playground

FIrst Edition

Gingko Press, Inc.
1321 Fifth Street
Berkeley, CA 94710, USA
Phone (510) 898 1195
Fax (510) 898 1196
email: books@gingkopress.com
www.gingkopress.com
ISBN: 978-1-58423-356-5

Printed in China

Credits
Written and edited by Evan Pricco
Additional writing by David Choe, Jeremy
Fish, Sam Flores, Ricky Powell, Munk One,
Estevan Oriol, Alex Pardee, Brian Flynn,
Dora Drimalas, Mike Giant, Usugrow and
Greg "Craola" Simkins

History by Matt Revelli and Adam Krohn

Primary photography by Jon Dragonette
Greg "Craola" Simkins photo by Jenn Simkins
Brian Flynn photo by Jeff Dey
Dora Drimalas photo by Leon Steel
Mike Giant photo by Jeff Luger
Alex Pardee photo by Kai Aitchison
Cover photo by Randy Dodson

Design by Hybrid Design, San Francisco
www.hybrid-design.com
Production by David Saavedra

UPPER PLAYGROUND
10 YEARS OF T-SHIRT GRAPHICS

NINE TEEN NINE TY NINE

99
DENIS KENNEDY
NICK LAWLER

Like most great business stories, this one begins in a garage. Circa 1999, the scene at the original UP headquarters was somewhat of an apartment, turned clubhouse, turned warehouse. Matt Revelli, the Creative Director of Upper Playground Enterprises, had racks upon racks in the garage, in his room, basically anywhere there was space for the few hundred T-shirts that seemed like an abundance of inventory at the time. The living room was the epicenter of it all. A few couches, recliners, some weights, and one of those gigantic 80's console TVs that takes 6 people to move, all set against the backdrop of a neon green wall with a Batman-esque walrus painted in black. This is where anything and everything UP happened early on, from strategy, to early photoshoots, to sorting T-shirts.

The first Upper Playground T-shirts were designed by Denis Kennedy. The first graphic consisted of five silhouetted breakdancing characters in various stages of breaking with different bright colors behind each character. Inspired from the sleeve of an old K-TEL record, this type of graphic was still relatively innovative at the time, DJ and breakdance graphics were still viable, and there really wasn't the mindnumbing abundance of T-shirts and T-shirt companies that you find today. The first UP catalog was Winter/Spring 1999; it was 1 page and consisted of 12 products. The tagline for that year was "Wear what you dig." Fast forward 10 years to the Spring 2009 catalog, a bi-annual, 175 page, perfect bound book, showcasing over 250 different products from over 60 artists from around the world.

The original Upper Playground retail store still thrives at 220 Fillmore Street, in the lower Haight neighborhood of San Francisco. The shop was originally a record store called Persimmon records. The back two rooms, which are still there today, consisted of Upper Playground on the right and American Junkies on the left. Fairly soon after American Junkies moved out, the owner of Persimmon unexpectedly retired, packed a bag and left for Hawaii. This left UP, still in it's infancy, with the entire retail store and over 200,000 records. The difference between records, and good records, is significant, both financially as well as physically. The good records never really made it out on the floor. With most of the Persimmon employees being DJ's, it was a rare occasion that they let a nice piece of vinyl slip past them. UP tried to keep the record store going at first, but after a while boxes of records would just be put out front on the street for people to take. Most people flipped through them, then passed, resulting in further

1999 Upper Playground logo
by **Denis Kennedy**

transporting, and various disposal methods. The back injuries sustained during this time period still take their toll on surviving members today.

Once the Fillmore Street basement was finally cleared, dozens of racks were installed, a couple steel desks brought in, a computer, and of course, the new TV, which stayed on for about 3 years straight. It was the centerpiece of the basement, on top of a linoleum covered table, where Matt Yep made sure every stack of shirts was folded with military precision. Originally, there were only a few staff members running the whole operation, each person doing what they needed to do and then having to do what-ever was not getting done. The retail store was often run by default, with sort of a "Hot Potato" mentality. If you were upstairs at the register, you could be stuck there for hours, that is, until someone else wandered up. Asking them to cover you for a second for a bathroom break, really meant, "Good luck, sucker....." and now it became their turn to man the register. In the early days, hours and hours could go by before a single customer would come through. There was very little retail in what was still a fairly unpolished neighborhood, very different than what you see today.

When Upper Playground was at its beginning stages, Revelli was working as a valet at an upscale San Francisco restaurant. A co-worker who parked with him had begun his own apparel company a few years prior, and every night in between parking cars, Revelli would grill him on all the various ins and outs of starting an apparel company: distribution production, costs, inventory, etc. The co-worker's response everyday was, "Don't do it. It's the shittiest business you could ever get involved with. Don't you see that I started a clothing company and I'm still working nights parking cars? It's not worth it." Revelli, who has a tendency to try and do things that people tell him are impossible, took his advice as positive reinforcement that this was exactly what he wanted to do. A couple of years after starting Upper Playground, Revelli remembers running into this former co-worker, who asked what was going on. Revelli told him, confidently, knowing that he would get a rise at his response, "I'm running my own apparel company." The response was simply "The fact that you didn't listen to a fucking thing I said is an indication that you might actually have what it takes to pull it off. You're stubborn and you don't take no for an answer, so at least you've got that going for you. Good luck." Hopefully, he gets his hands on a copy of this book, wherever he may be these days........

UPPER PLAYGROUND

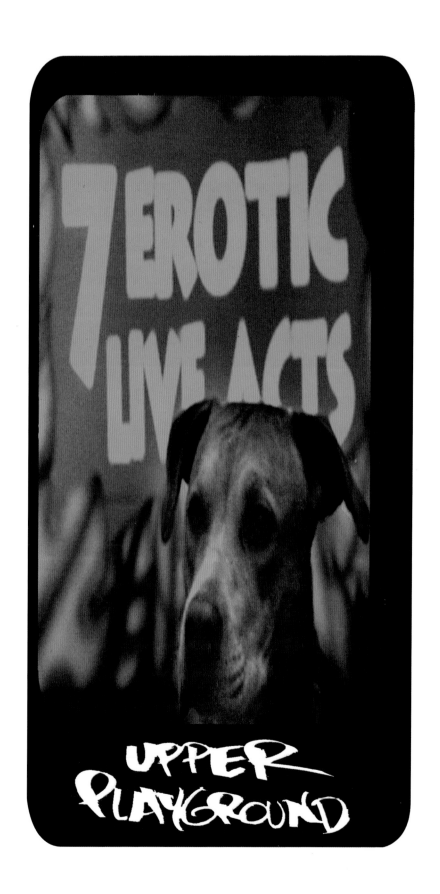

game program™
upper playground
UP-1979

1-5	TANK®
6-9	TANK-PONG™
10-14	INVISIBLE-TANK™
15-20	BIPLANE
21-27	JET-FIGHTER™

Use with Joystick Controllers

UPPER
PLAYGROUND™

TWØ THØUS AND

00
DENIS KENNEDY
DAMON SOULE
SHEPARD FAIREY
DAVE KINSEY

By early 2000, Upper Playground stickers were literally everywhere in San Francisco and the Bay Area. These were all of the original UP logo - an oval shape with a sketched walrus and cursive "Upper Playground" scribbled below. Admittedly, most people who saw the stickers had absolutely no idea what Upper Playground was, including current Director of Operations, Adam Krohn (AK), who started seeing these stickers slapped all over the city. For every sticker that fell victim to the "buff," at least 50 more would go up. This statistic did not change for quite sometime.

As AK remembers, his first understanding of Upper Playground as a clothing brand, was at the Magic and ASR trade shows in 2000. Most brands attending these shows gave off more of a corporate business vibe, or at least looked like they were trying to write some orders. But then there was Upper Playground, with a gigantic crew of friends from what looked like completely different cliques, just hanging out in the smallest booth one could possibly have. With two of the largest DJs (in terms of physical size, Frank and Serge) from San Francisco spinning records and many members of the UP sponsored skate team, it was hard to figure out if anything was actually for sale. The image they gave to the rest of the show was that of a posse, without a businessperson in sight.

AK remembers walking by their booth at one point, and the skate team was rolling in a bunch of flat screen TVs to be used as color monitors at the booth. At that time monitors were sort of a status symbol at tradeshows, with only the heavily financed brands participating in the video-flexing game, but here was Upper Playground, presenting themselves as larger-than-life. They had color catalogs, monitors at the booth; one could almost conclude that they looked like the "real deal." Of course, in what was a signature UP maneuver, the brand new TVs were returned to Best Buy after the show for a full refund after presenting the carefully protected receipt. One thing that was not a façade was the diversity of the crew; there were the skate kids, graffiti artists, DJ's and the fine artists all hanging out together. In 2000, it was still rare to have such a wide-ranging group of people enjoying their similarities rather than focusing on their differences. Today, it's so common to see that diversity that you could forget how separate those groups were less than a decade ago.

When those shows were over, AK began to see Upper Playground merchandise in some small stores around San Francisco. It wasn't until later that he heard that

2000 Upper Playground logo
by **Denis Kennedy**

UP was beginning to do TV commercials, or should we say, attempting to film commercials. This was another instance of hiring Barbizon models, sometimes even strippers, to film in Chinatown late into the night. Revelli had another job as a bouncer at a club, and remembers having to leave in the middle of the video shoot to go to the nightclub. Not only was UP doing standout marketing schemes at the trade shows, definitely the first to bring live painting, but they were also getting into TV commercials. What small apparel company filmed commercials? In the early '90's, none. They ended up airing as local commercial spots on MTV at the highly rated hours between 2-4 AM, a true remnant airtime bargain.

Needless to say, Upper Playground left an impression on people at those early shows, and to Krohn especially. These experiences created momentum and energy, and it appeared that the company had money (which they didn't) and that they were on to something that might actually catch on in the apparel game (which they were). One thing was obvious, though, in order to run a small apparel company, you had to get up, get over, and work every angle you could just to make it to the next season, hoping that someday you would make it to the promised land of "getting paid."

12

**DENIS
KENNEDY**

13

**DENIS
KENNEDY**

14

**DENIS
KENNEDY**

DENIS
KENNEDY

DENIS
KENNEDY

DENIS
KENNEDY

DENIS
KENNEDY

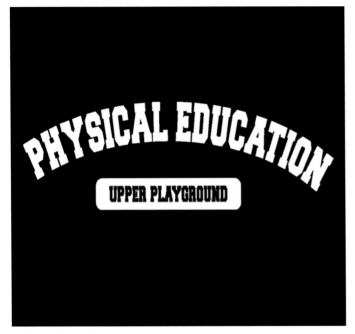

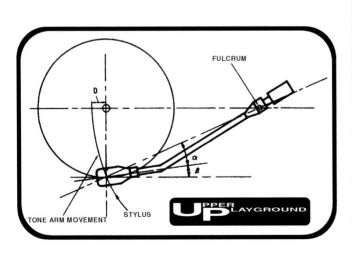

25
**DENIS
KENNEDY**

26
**DENIS
KENNEDY**

27
**DENIS
KENNEDY**

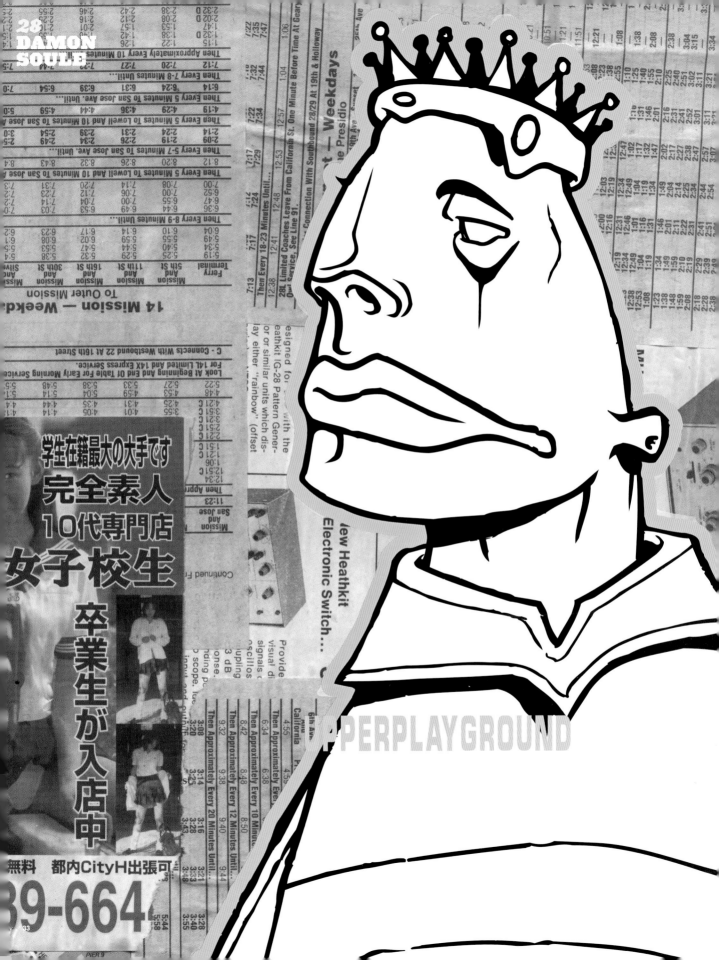

TWØ THØUS AND ØNE

01

DENIS KENNEDY
DAMON SOULE
DALE DRIELING
GREG CHAUSPAIT
CHRIS PASTRAS
RICKY POWELL
SAM FLORES
AM RADIO
ART NOMAD

On September 11, 2001, a lone shopper wandered into the store and purchased a T-shirt. The Fillmore Street store was, of course, open for the entire day that Tuesday. There was a strict policy that the store was to remain open every day of the year, except for Columbus Day, some sort of Italian mandate. Yet, the man who bought the tee on 9/11 was completely aware of what had happened earlier that day, but he still just wanted to buy that shirt. This seemed like some sort of sign that if the apocalypse were to happen, people might still buy T's on their way out.

Revelli remembers of this time, "Everybody immediately dismissed the idea, were unimpressed, or didn't understand what UP was doing. Today, put-ting art-heavy graphics on tees is all there is. It is amazing how the tides have changed; only eight years ago, nobody gave a shit."

By the middle of 2001, things were picking up for the brand. They had built a strong relationship with customers in Japan, which really carried the brand in the first few years. The UP staff traveled to Japan often, trying to figure out what was going on over there, while the Japanese were simultaneously doing the same over here. At this point the Japanese were still really into American street culture, which they would soon transform into a style of their own. For the time being, however, their unquenchable thirst for the US look financed the UP brand expansion for the first 3-4 years.

Watching domestic and international sales steadily grow, it was time to turn the momentum back to Fillmore Street. The first thought on local expansion was to create a gallery space to showcase the artists responsible for the graphics that made these T-shirts so different. The UP team had begun to see that something lacked in the general public's understanding of the concept of fine art on a T-shirt, as most brands were not showcasing contemporary art pieces on T's yet. By showing a customer the art in its original form through a gallery setting, it was concluded that it would help hype both the artist and the brand. Understanding the story behind each T-shirt meant understanding the larger picture that Upper Playground was trying to deliver.

Revelli found a space that had been an upholstery shop for over 100 years, which could have been condemned by the health department. It was a dis-gusting, unsafe, dilapidated excuse for a building, with cheap rent and conve-niently located next door to 220 Fillmore...This read as "perfect" for the UP real estate team. A friend of the UP family, Mickey Lawler, had shown extreme enthusiasm about the space and had a background in construction. Lawler wanted to have his own solo show, and it was told to him, "You fix up this space, you get the first show at FIFTY24SF Gallery."

Therefore, in 2001, the first show ever to be held at the FIFTY24SF Gal-

2001 Upper Playground logo
by **Denis Kennedy**

lery was with a non-artist, Mickey Lawler, consisting of found photography. Not just any found photography either - somehow, at the dump, he got his hands on an archive of stock airline employee manual photos. Basically stewards showing airline food, smiling in the aisles, doing the pre-flight instructions, all extremely staged, albeit typical, airline "moments." Lawler took all the found photos, blew them up in large format until they were at least 3-feet x 4- feet, probably spending over $5,000 on just that portion of the show. What put the show over the top was Lawler's improv routine, presenting each picture by really trying to get into the mind of, and explain, the photographed subject, all of this through a fuzzy micro-phone feed and the roar of the audience. In hindsight, this first show was probably pound for pound one of the best that FIFTY24SF Gallery has ever had, and the only one worthy of an encore performance. Somehow, the original framed photos mysteriously appeared in 2006 to grace the walls of the retail store.

Lawler was a dedicated UP family member through and through, who was obsessed with upping the brand all over the greater Bay Area. At one point, Lawler decided to wheat paste the entirety of his Ford Ranger with Upper Playground logos, hubcaps and tires included. Other than the windshield and side windows, it was all logos, the original "wrapped" vehicle. The Ranger was worth about $1,000, but in-side, there was this massive $5,000 stereo system. As positive consequence for UP, Lawler would drive up and down Haight Street, put on his creepers, blast his Jamaican "Sound system" music, driving 5 MPH up and down Haight Street all day. Sometimes if he felt up to it Lawler would cover the entire Bay Area, adding a deeper degree of public confusion to what the Walrus actually represented. In the end it seems appropriate that Lawler was the first show at the FIFTY24SF Gallery space.

After only a handful of shows, FIFTY24SF Gallery was listed in a local San Francisco weekly paper as the "Best Gallery to Get Drunk At." There was a rather large and intimidating gentleman named Isaac working the door. He really took his job seriously, and once the space hit capacity, no one else was let in. This would surprise visiting artists when they couldn't go back in their own show and even more surprised UP staff when they couldn't go into their own gallery. It was Isaac's door. After some fights, public urinations, and realization that the art had become secondary to whatever free booze the sponsoring alcohol company was trying to promote, the era of the open bar came to an end. It was for the best for everyone involved.

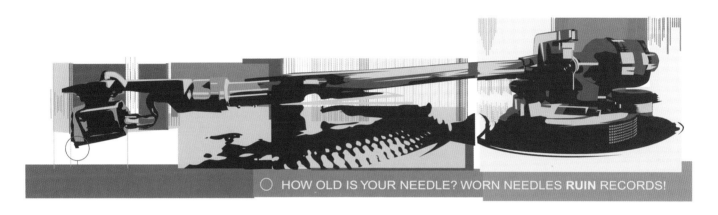

○ HOW OLD IS YOUR NEEDLE? WORN NEEDLES **RUIN** RECORDS!

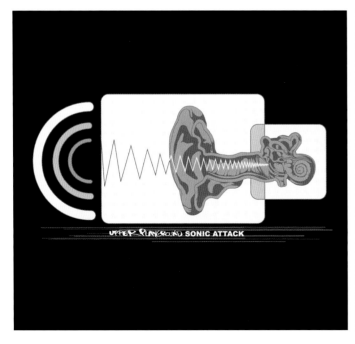

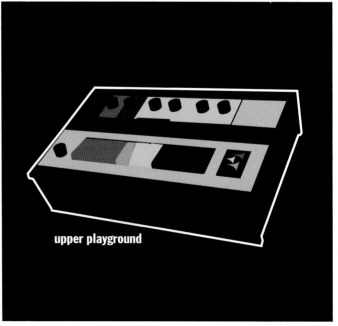

AUDIO FILES

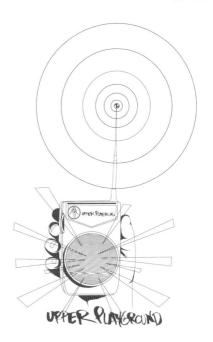

UPPER PLAYGROUND

40
DENIS KENNEDY

41
DALE DRIELING

42
GREG CHAVSPAIT

43
CHRIS PASTRAS

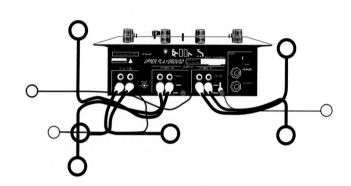

UPPERPLAYGROUND
SECURITY PROTOTYPE MODEL 4203P

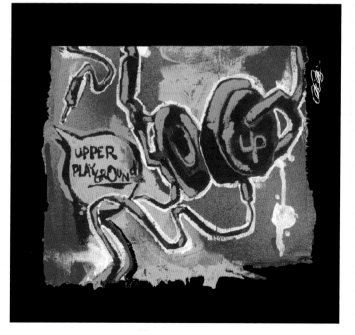

UPPER PLAYGROUND

LONG PLAYING ORIGINAL

When I did my first UP designs I had no experience with Illustrator or computers in general. I remember turning in the drawings in blue ballpoint pen. At that time UP was really small; they had a tiny catalog no wider then a Garfield comic book, with maybe six designs in it. I went to visit them at their headquarters/live-in party house. When you walked in the back dorm room there was a huge TV with skate stickers and tags all over it, a bench press in the living room, and stack of pizza boxes as a coffee table. In the kitchen they had milk crates stacked up six-feet high, where they kept their inventory. That was the original Upper Playground. It was a completely different scene than you see today.

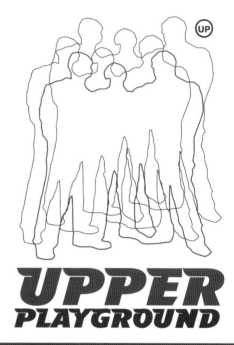

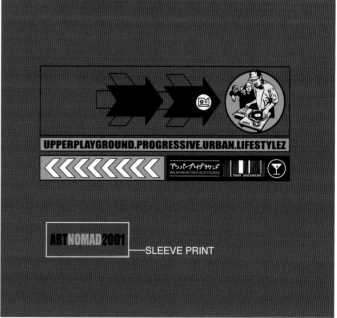

" Get Zooted ! "

Upper Pla

ground

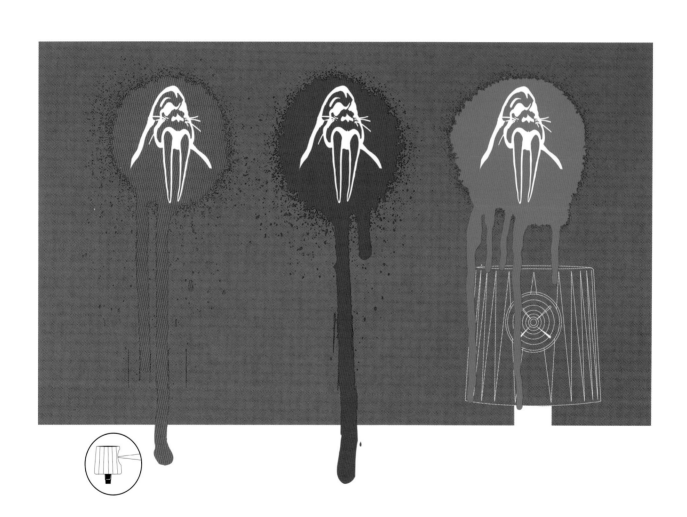

DENIS
KENNEDY

DENIS
KENNEDY

DENIS
KENNEDY

DENIS
KENNEDY

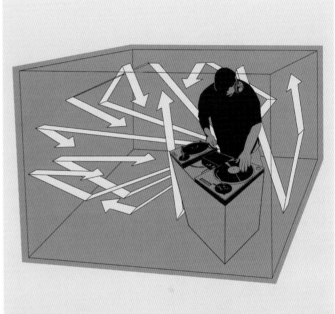

TWO THOUS AND TWO

As has been the case at the beginning of each year, Upper Playground started 2002 close to being bankrupt. There came a point that even with Japanese sales going fairly well, UP desperately needed to get themselves more customers and more accounts so they could stay alive for another season. One brainstorm, that became a reality in 3 phone calls, was to get a Chevy Suburban and drive across the country and back. The simple objective was to sticker and wheat paste the hell out of every place they could, pick up some more accounts, and further build Upper Playground's name outside of the Bay Area.

Enter J. McCain. To most people associated with him, McCain was perhaps the biggest character of the early UP years. He was the most hardcore, passionate, driven person of the UP family; McCain would even shame Revelli, boldly stating that even he was not doing enough to make this company a profitable, household name. McCain would shame everyone, in fact. Not a physically big man, his personality was what became larger than life, and nothing would get in his way if he had a mission or a goal in mind. He was so determined to make Upper Playground a success that he would do anything, ANYTHING, to make it happen. There were never enough stickers to go up, there was never an impossible spot to wheatpaste, and because of this diehard nature, he was the original member of the team, along with Eddie Gutierrez, to get the proverbial "ups" for making UP work. He was the nonstop promotional machine.

You couldn't stop him. He was, without a doubt, "The Terminator" of guerilla marketing, as well as the first official sales person.

The grand scheme of the trip was for McCain, UP contributor and photographer, Dylan Maddux, and Revelli to print thousands and thousands of Upper Playground stickers and posters to wheatpaste, rent the Suburban , and start driving across the country trying to get new stores to carry UP. They planned a journey going from San Francisco to the East coast then down to the Dirty South, and back west to the Bay Area. It was a make-it or break-it trip, the first in a reoccurring, but necessary, series of make-it or break-it trips that defined UP during the first few years.

One of the more successful ideas for getting the UP name out there was born from McCain. He came up with the genius idea that he entitled "Loud Mouth Promotion." It was self-explanatory. McCain would go into a crowded area, store, or public event anywhere in the United States, get himself somehow elevated above the pack, and henceforth scream, "UPPER PLAAAAAYGROUND!!!!" at the top of his lungs, repeatedly, until the entire universe heard or paid attention to him. Imagine a mall in Kansas, people shopping or eating cinnamon buns at the food court, and J. McCain standing on a table screaming "Upper Playground" over and over again. It's infectious, or annoying. But it works. There was another method McCain used as well: Upon meeting new people he would not use common courtesies such as, "hello," or "nice to meet you." No, he would, almost like a possessed doll, repeat "Upper Playground" over and over, substituting every phrase or word in the English language for the two most important to him: "Upper" and "Playground." This determination and devotion to the brand was great when a spot needed to get bombed with a wheat-pasted UP logo, and of course great when an entire mall in the Midwest that needed to be vocally assaulted by three men from San Francisco.

At one point on the trip, the unfortunate happened. McCain got arrested. He didn't have a driver's license, so the only time he was called upon to drive was in Atlanta, Georgia. As soon as he got behind the wheel and left the parking lot, probably less than a minute after, according to Revelli, McCain was pulled over for no turn signal and was promptly arrested. After a brief scramble to scrounge up $500 to bail him out, the crew got back on the road, opting for the quickest route home.

When driving back to SF from the South, in the midst of a crazy storm, an icicle somehow fell from a power line that crossed over the Interstate highway, and promptly shattered the windshield of the vehicle. What are the odds that an icicle hits a moving object going 80 MPH? The rental car company informed them that it was, indeed, quite rare, nearly impossible. It was going to take too long to get a new car, so the rental car people begrudgingly let the team of three drive from Kansas City back to SF. With their heads out the side windows, these worn out road warriors did their best to avoid any more jailtime or damage to the car for the next 36 hours. McCain ended up kicking out the windshield at some point, thus restoring some sense of normalcy for the remaining drive.

In the end, the trip proved to be successful for UP. Many of the staff think that because of it, 2002 was the year UP truly entered the game. They built relationships with stores outside of the Bay Area, creating more funds, allowing them to develop catalogs for multiple seasons. The momentum was just continually being built, but it didn't take away from the fact that UP was always on the brink of being bankrupt or of having everything fall apart. But this trip got them past "Stage 1."

It was wheat-pasting and getting the message out that really got Upper Playground through the first years. When you're getting up and constantly pushing to make the impossible predicament succeed, taking trips across the US and hitting every spot you can with your logo, you are telling every naysayer that you are not fucking playing around.

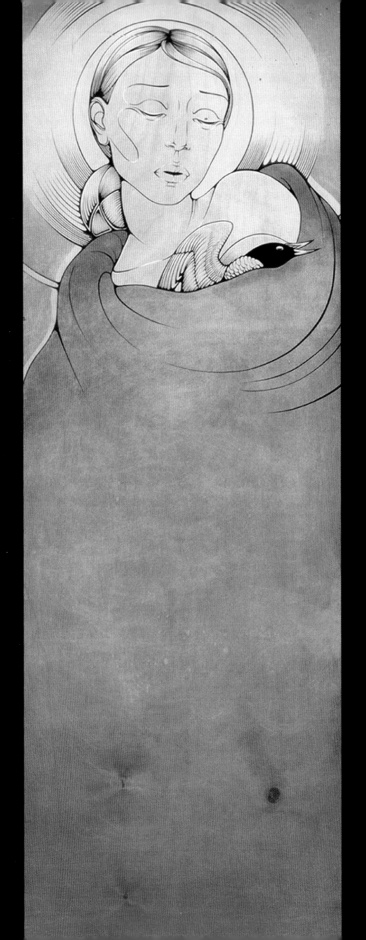

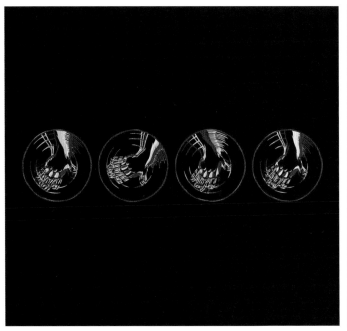

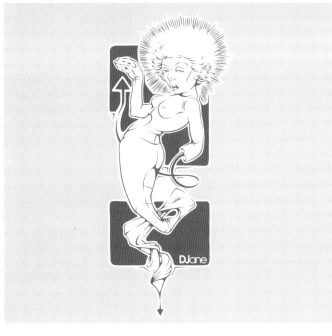

upper playground

69
SAM
FLORES

70
SAM
FLORES

71
SAM
FLORES

72
SAM
FLORES

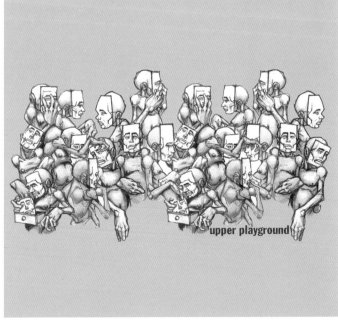

SAM
FLORES

SAM
FLORES

SAM
FLORES

upper playground

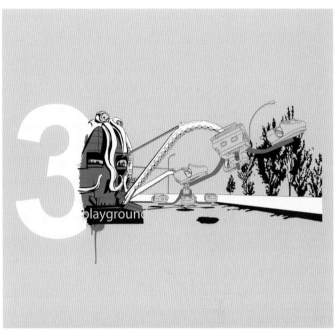

76
SAM
FLORES

77
SAM
FLORES

78
SAM
FLORES

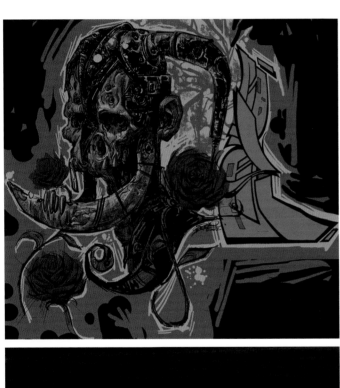

82
RICKY
POWELL

83
RICKY
POWELL

84
RICKY
POWELL

KEEPIN' IT REAL...

ZOOTED

Ricky Powell

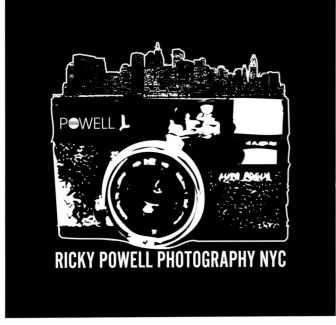

NO GAME →

31
RICKY
POWELL

32
RICKY
POWELL

33
RICKY
POWELL

SCRUB →

SiD - 13 St. PARK NYC

SAMFLORES:

Ricky Powell

96
RICKY
POWELL X
REVOLT

97
RICKY
POWELL X
MICHELLE
TARANTELLI

98
RICKY
POWELL

99
RICKY
POWELL X
KIERNEN

100
AM
RADIO

101
AM
RADIO

102
AM
RADIO

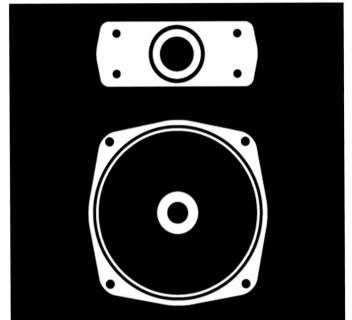

UPPER PL

YGROUND

104
DENIS KENNEDY

105
DENIS KENNEDY

106
DENIS KENNEDY

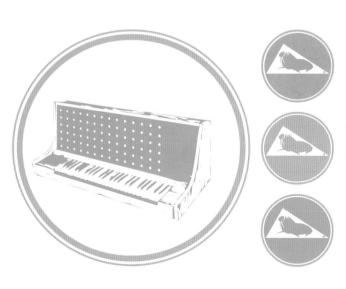

107
DENIS
KENNEDY

108
DENIS
KENNEDY

109
DENIS
KENNEDY

110
DENIS
KENNEDY

111
**BRYCE
KANIGHTS**

112
**ANDY
JENKINS**

113
**CHRIS
PASTRAS**

© BRYCE KANIGHTS

MARK GONZALES
"ALCATRAZ"
1988

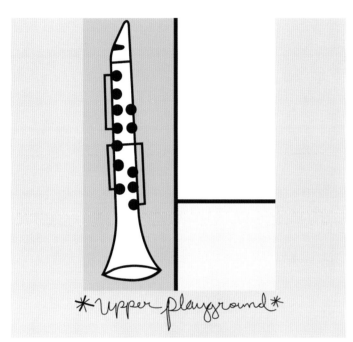

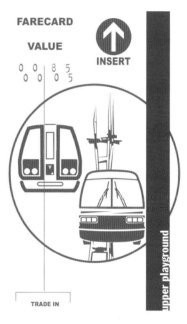

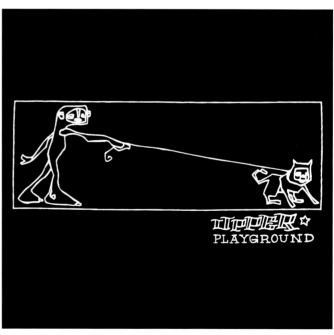

For me, it's still about "getting up." Since day one, T-shirts have been a way for me to get my work out to the general public in a wearable, affordable way. Just like each tag is out there building my rep, so is every T-shirt. I'm just glad I was involved in UP early on. It's been great to see the brand grow over the last 10 years. It's also been really great knowing Matt and Upper Playground. I see them as a peer not just in business, but life in general.

118
**GIANT
ONE**

119
**GIANT
ONE**

120
**IAN
JOHNSON**

129
**JEREMY
FISH**

130
**DAVID
CHOE**

131
**DAVID
CHOE**

TWØ THØUS AND THREE

03

RICKY POWELL
COLIN MILLER
ANDY HOWELL
CHRIS LINDIG
AMAZE
ANDY MUELLER
ANDY JENKINS
DAVID CHOE
DUG ONE
RON ENGLISH
DAVE SCHUBERT
DENIS KENNEDY
DORA DRIMALAS
ZEPHYR
CASTLE CPH
LONDON POLICE
STASH
RICH JACOBS
JO JACKSON
JEREMY FISH
GREG GALINSKY
GIANT ONE
TIFFANY BOZIC
BRIAN FLYNN
SAM FLORES
ALBERT REYES
BIGFOOT
GREY
CODY HUDSON

If there are two themes that could encapsulate Upper Playground in its first 5 years, the first is that they were always working an angle to get something for free, cheap, discounted, or playing a situation to their advantage. The flipside of this, theme two, is that if something could go wrong, it most definitely always would. Somehow, and from the lips of someone (to remain nameless) who runs the company, there was karma that had to be fought off.

As was the case the previous year (and every year), 2003 found UP needing to expand its brand recognition out to the rest of North America and into more stores ideally result-ing in new orders, more orders and re-orders. The idea was that AK would go to the Midwest, Canada, and into the East to create and build relationships with more accounts. This trip, however, was going to be a bit more thought out: a list of stores was made, a map dotted, some arbitrary pathway starting in Detroit across the US and Canada was drawn, and AK got on his way.

This is where the afore-mentioned themes play a role in the story. The angle was that UP had a hook-up at a Detroit area Enterprise Rent-A-Car, which meant they had the "friends and family" rate along with healthy upgrades. AK departed San Francisco promised either a Benz or a Lincoln Town Car for the trip. However, upon arrival in Detroit, AK was welcomed to a dreary scene: only one car was left avail-able on the entire lot. And that car was a gold-colored, anti-luxury, Saturn sedan. Thus was born what is more commonly known in UP circles as, "The Gold Saturn Trip."

The company consisted of only four or five people at this point, so being on the road meant that AK was still obligated to remotely take care of his daily duties at UP. Even though we are talking about 2003, there was yet to be full wireless access all over the Ameri-can landscape; you had to stop somewhere to use the Internet (Holiday Inns, truck stops, those sorts of locations). AK remembers getting calls 15 times a day dealing with UP at home, while trying to get to more stores on the road. Revelli claimed it was like the whole company was on pause when he left town. (To this day the company still operates in the sense that losing one person to a vacation or business trip can throw things off for the entire office. Locating a missing box of T's or a particular graphic file can become an odyssey.)

"The Gold Saturn Trip" went well in the sense that AK met good people, built relations, and was able to get UP product into some of the best stores on

UPPER
PLAYGROUND

2003 Upper Playground logo
by **Brian Flynn**

their wish list. Sometimes he would walk into a store as a random customer and not tell anyone who he was, be given the "attitude", and never sell to them again, without explanation. Most stores, though, would be really excited and would even tell him, "No brand has ever visited our store, ever." In some instances, he would go into a store and not believe what the hell was going on. One store, somewhere in western North Carolina, literally sold only Pelle Pelle and Pakistani porn videotapes, but had managed to buy some shirts from UP at one point. As AK puts it, "It was probably the sketchiest place I had ever been."

AK's arbitrarily drawn pathways had him driving from Detroit to Montreal, down to Charlotte, up to Indianapolis, to Milwaukee, and then back to Detroit. He ended up visiting three stores a day, building amazing relationships throughout the entire journey. By seeing the store, meeting the owner and understanding the neighborhood, it became so much easier to do business with these accounts. This sort of attention to detail was of benefit, as Upper Playground still has over half of those customers today. This was another case of 4th quarter heroics by the brand, allowing for the bills to get paid and for another season to get put out.

Even though securing stores and attracting new customers was advancing at a comfortable pace, UP needed to gain some bigger customers to push them over the top into continuous streams of financial revenue (coincidently, they are still looking for this to happen in 2009). In one of their more innovative advertising schemes UP took out ads in various magazines, soliciting the buyer of Urban Outfitters to call them for business. The ad had a picture of an open matchbook with the name of the UO buyer on the back of it, asking her by name to "Please call us," at Upper Playground. Nobody had ever done an ad like this, and the Urban Outfitters buyer even saw it. It was heard that they had the ad up in their lunchroom for a long time. Things really started to get fun at this point, when UP began to realize they could do whatever they wanted, and didn't have to follow some sort of industry standard. Still working the angles. Making any situation, whether taking an ad or renting a car, work to your immediate advantage. Sometimes you get the gold Saturn, sometimes you get the gold.

133
RICKY
POWELL

134
RICKY
POWELL

135
RICKY
POWELL

136
RICKY
POWELL

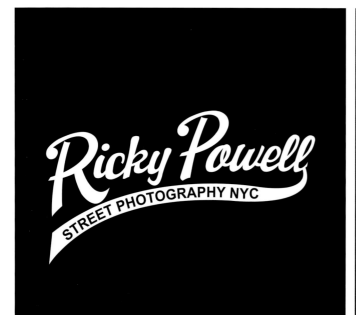

FUNKY DOPE MANUEVERS

139
RICKY
POWELL

140
RICKY
POWELL

ALL YOU NEED IS A
P H D

PETE MARAVICH
FREAKS

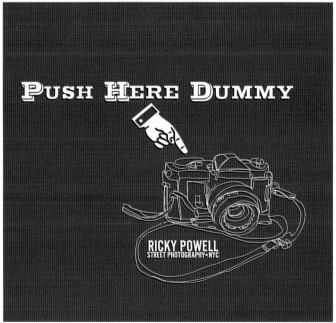

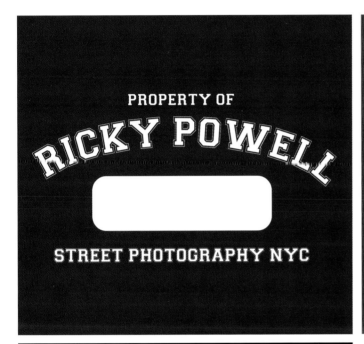

145
RICKY POWELL X DK

146
RICKY POWELL X DK

147
RICKY POWELL X DK

148
RICKY POWELL X DK

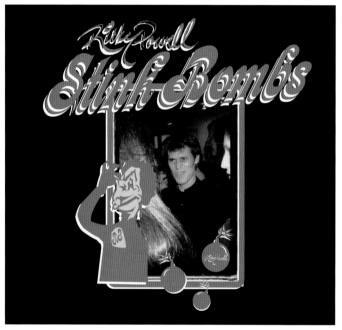

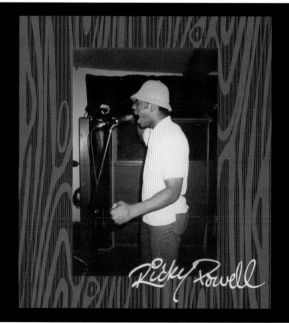

151
RICKY POWELL

152
RICKY POWELL

153
RICKY POWELL

154
RICKY POWELL

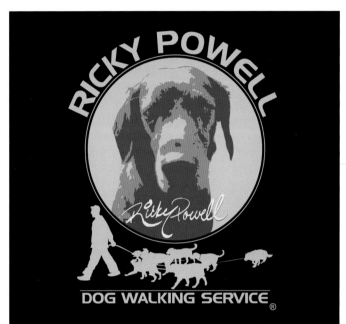

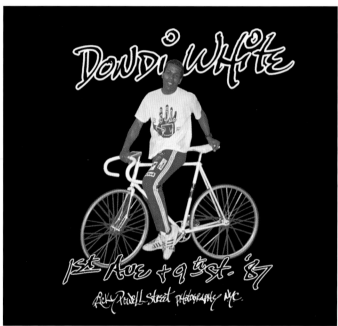

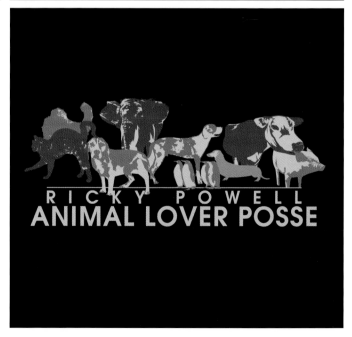

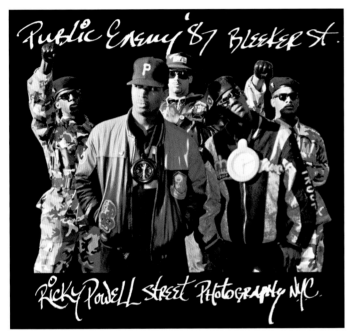

159
CHRIS LINDIG

160
CHRIS LINDIG

161
INJUN

162
AMAZE

164
**ANDY
MUELLER**

165
**ANDY
MUELLER**

166
**ANDY
MUELLER**

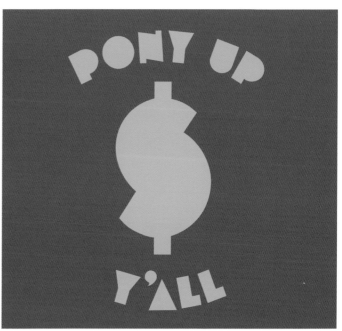

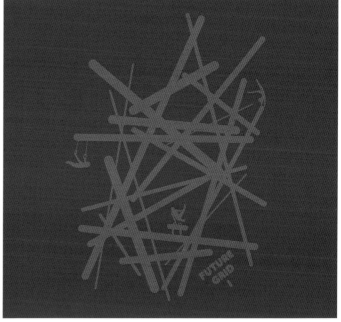

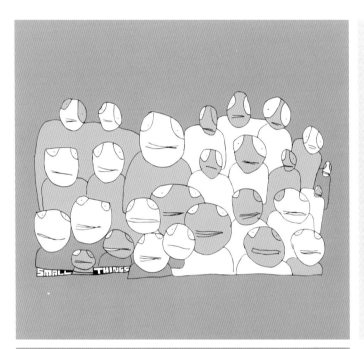

170
**DAVID
CHOE**

171
**DAVID
CHOE**

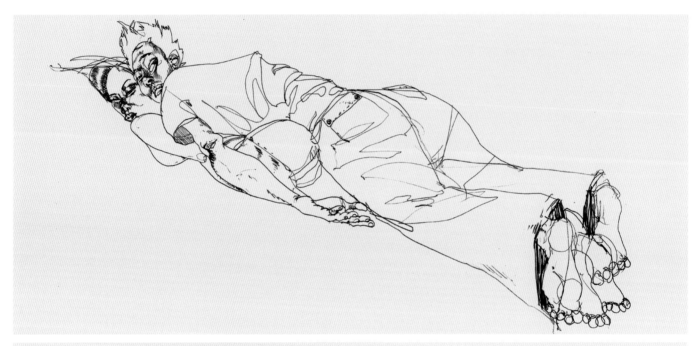

DENIS
KENNEDY

DENIS
KENNEDY

DENIS
KENNEDY

DENIS
KENNEDY

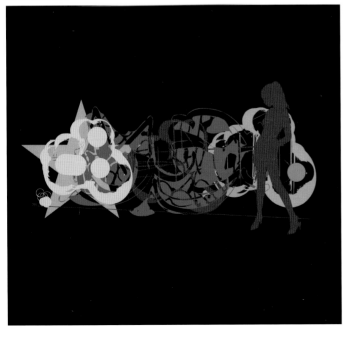

181
DENIS KENNEDY

182
DENIS KENNEDY

183
DENIS KENNEDY

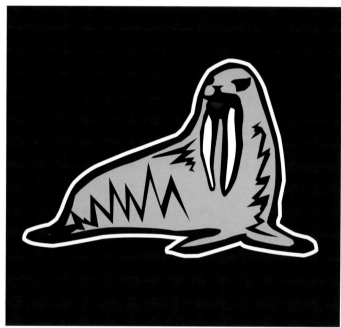

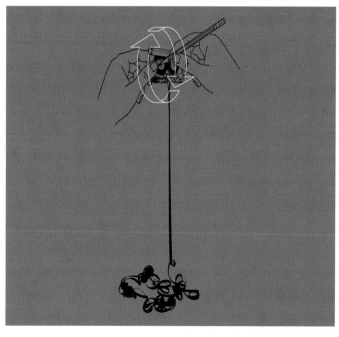

184

DENIS
KENNEDY

185

DENIS
KENNEDY

186

DAVE
SCHUBERT

187

DAVE
SCHUBERT

188
DENIS
KENNEDY

189
DENIS
KENNEDY

190
DENIS
KENNEDY

191
DENIS
KENNEDY

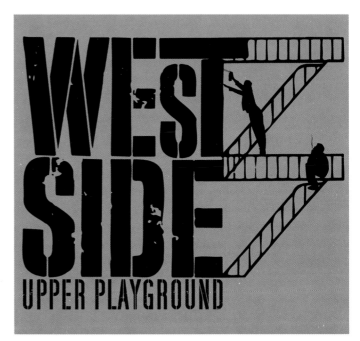

DORA
DRIMALAS

DORA
DRIMALAS

DORA
DRIMALAS

DORA
DRIMALAS

196
DUG ONE

197
DUG ONE

198
DUG ONE

199
RON ENGLISH

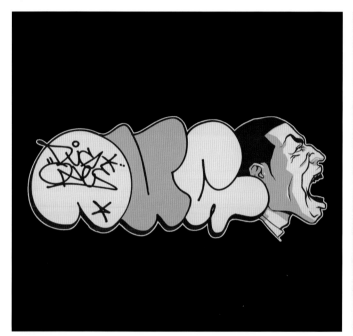

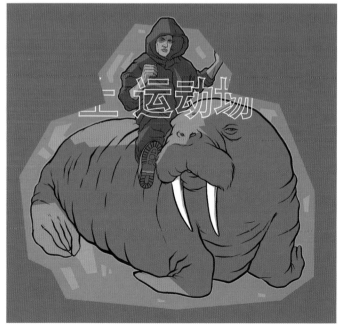

MC SUPERSIZED

201
ZEPHYR

202
ZEPHYR

203
CASTLE CPH

204
CASTLE CPH

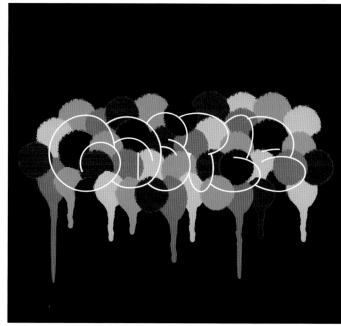

Initially, my tees didn't sell well at all. I think Matt and Adam just liked me so they let me have a shirt or two in the catalog for a LOOOONG time before anyone was really buying my stuff. I remember making a funny gold chain with a middle finger medallion 5 or 6 years ago. I saw an OG Fillmore pimp-type dude, maybe 60 year-old, sporting it. Made me so fucking happy. It was funny, I swear.

209
JEREMY
FISH

210
JEREMY
FISH

211
JO
JACKSON

212
JO
JACKSON

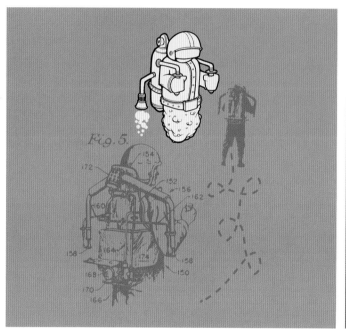

GREG
GALINSKY

GREG
GALINSKY

GIANT
ONE

GIANT
ONE

GIANT
ONE

GIANT
ONE

GIANT
ONE

221
**GIANT
ONE**

222
**TIFFANY
BOZIC**

223
**BRIAN
FLYNN**

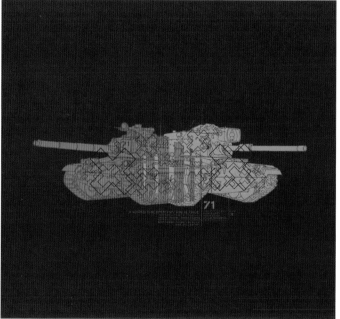

SAM
FLORES

SAM
FLORES

SAM
FLORES

SAM
FLORES

228
SAM FLORES

229
SAM FLORES

230
SAM FLORES

231
SAM FLORES

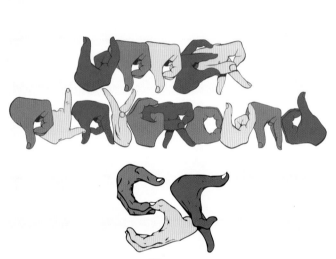

UPPER PLAYGROUND

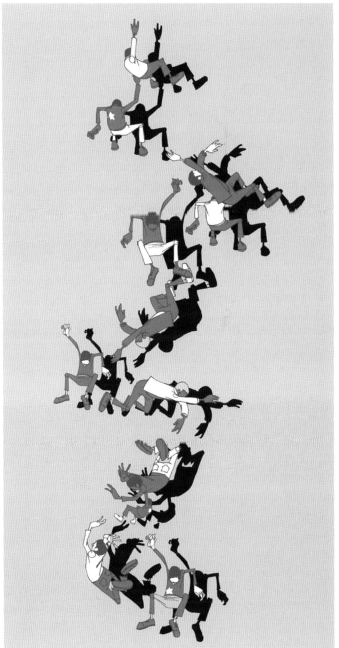

238
SAM FLORES

239
SAM FLORES

240
SAM FLORES

241
SAM FLORES

SAM
FLORES

SAM
FLORES

SAM
FLORES

245
SAM FLORES

246
SAM FLORES

247
SAM FLORES

248
SAM FLORES

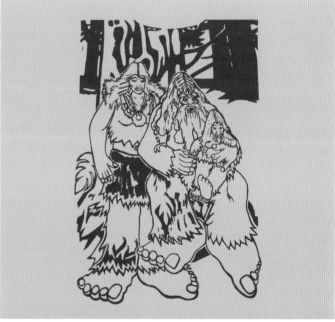

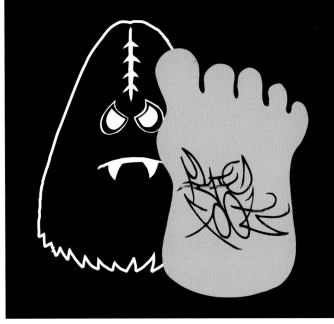

264
BIGFOOT

265
BIGFOOT

266
BIGFOOT

267
BIGFOOT

269
BIGFOOT

270
BIGFOOT

271
BIGFOOT

272
BIGFOOT

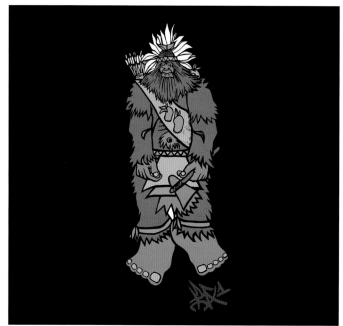

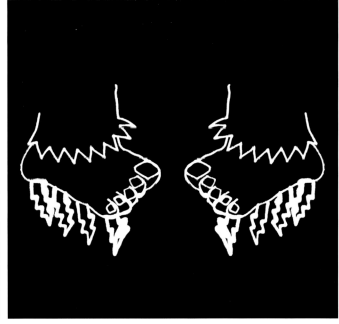

276
BIGFOOT

277
BIGFOOT

278
BIGFOOT

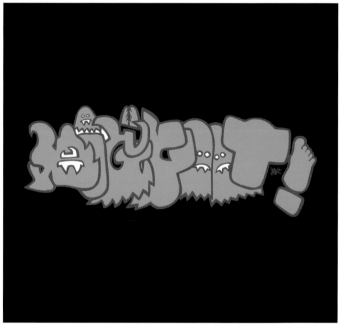

229
GREY

230
GREY

231
GREY

232
GREY

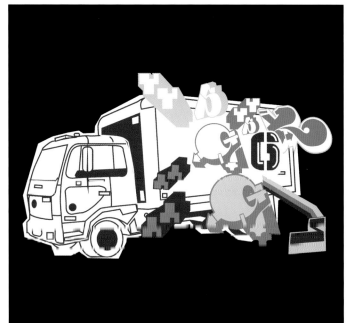

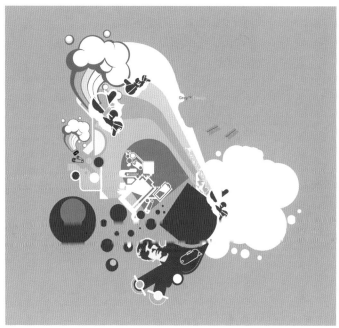

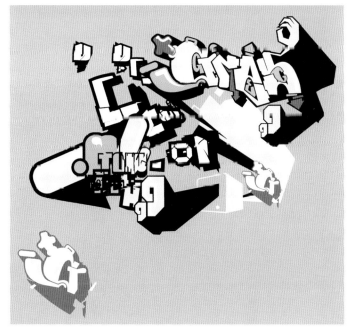

283
GREY

284
GREY

285
GREY

286
GREY

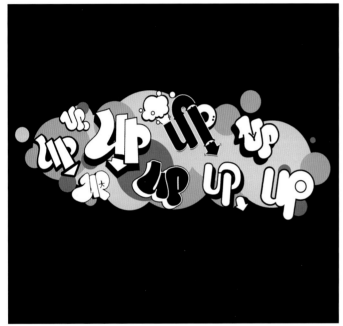

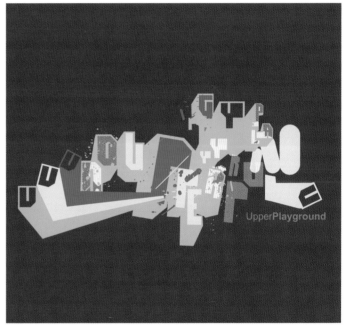

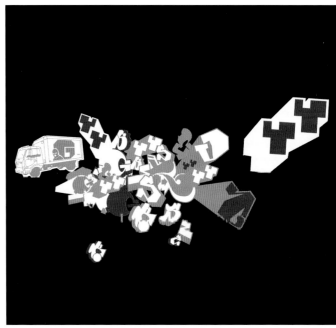

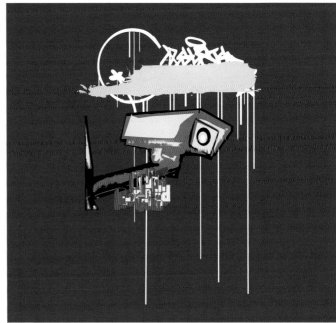

TWØ THØUS AND FØUR

04

ALBERT REYES
GIANT ONE
BIGFOOT
DENIS KENNEDY
KOFIE
CASTLE CPH
SAM FLORES
GREY
DWOK
BRIAN FLYNN
WILL BARRAS
LONDON POLICE
JEREMY FISH
DORA DRIMALAS
MR. JAGO
TASACO HASU
KUSTAA SASKI
DAVID CHOE
RICKY POWELL
JOHN DUDA
BRAD DIGITAL
JOKER
CORO
ANDY JENKINS
NOAH BUTKUS

NATE CRANE
MAT O'BRIEN
CHRIS SILVA
LOGAN HICKS
MORNING BREATH
DYLAN MADDUX
DAVE SCHUBERT
AIYANA UDESEN
COLIN MILLER
GALO
ANDY MUELLER
MAXUK
CODY HUDSON

The energy was definitely high as 2004 saw Dr Revolt and Zephyr paint the mural on the rooftop of the Fillmore Street store. Infamous NYC-based street photographer Ricky Powell introduced Upper Playground to the entire culture of luminary East Coast personalities that UP would undoubtedly otherwise never have had the chance to work with in the brand's infant stages. It was always felt that the roof piece was a pivotal moment for Upper Playground because, in a way, it was like a blessing for the brand from two kings of the NYC graffiti movement. Artists like Seen, Dondi, Zephyr, Revolt, Phil Frost, and Ramelzee, were combined with images of artists, like Basquiat, gracing T-shirts for the UP x Ricky Powell line. This truly helped mark a turning point in the brand's acceptance nationwide. Mr. Powell was able to get crucial East Coast validation early on for UP, which created a new wave of momentum for the brand.

AK remembers, "Ever since a certain album dropped in the summer of '89, you knew the name Ricky Powell. And when you work with Ricky, or just talk to him for a few minutes, you are all of a sudden in conversation with all your favorite graffiti artists, hip-hop musicians, and icons that made up the New York City scene that all of us at Upper Playground were growing up with and had been truly affected by. Ricky has a story to go with everything; whether it was a tour stop in Oakland with Public Enemy in 1988, or catching Andy Warhol and Basquiat walking in SoHo, each photo that we put on a T-shirt was a time capsule into a time that was part of the major inspiration and the origins of UP. Ricky made you feel like you were there."

With that idea of storytelling in mind, UP wanted to document the art and artists that they had been working alongside for the first half-decade of the company. As history proved, there hadn't been many documentaries made on the subject and, as Revelli puts it, "We didn't feel that a lot of people had actually seen many of the graffiti and fine artists whose art was on our T's and in our gallery." The UP-produced documentary, "Dithers," was a behind-the-scenes look at the art which pushed the movement which consistently inspired the brand. It also captured the essence of these artists that worked with UP or had been major personalities in the contemporary art world even if they didn't work with the brand. UP had the experiences of hanging out with a lot of these people already; traveling with them, talking before and after shows, or watching their process to complete work.

Revelli learned that

when you spent a significant amount of time with artists, the paintings took on a whole new meaning, and you began to see what this entire movement and the people who participated in it were really all about. "Dithers" took the concept of the arts and artists being able to express themselves in words, to take the experience of what UP was seeing on a personal level, and open that up to thousands of people. Art, especially graffiti and street art, can be somewhat anonymous, with a rare chance to ever see the person or get the story behind a process. "Dithers" was that window into these personalities and stories. There was the graphic artist, graffiti writer,

photographer, illustrator, and fine artist - everyone together telling their stories. Most of them had yet to be given their due respect and to be put into a historical context of what was happening in the underground contemporary art scene that had been gaining energy in the late 1990s and early '00s.

At first nobody wanted to participate in the making of "Dithers." The artists were hesitant, especially the graffiti writers, because for this generation, a documentary on this particular group of artists had never been done. There were no blueprints or past knowledge of the repercussions for showing their faces on film and to

explain what they were doing. A lot of these people were unknown outside of their artistic imagery, and this was the first time they were going to be physically seen. Upper Playground believed that there existed a dedicated audience that would follow a film project of this importance. In consequence, "Dithers" allowed UP expansion into other fields besides just apparel and gallery shows. By the time "Dithers" was completed, more and more artists wanted to be in the next documentary that was going to be produced. By the time "Dithers" was in post-production, "The Run Up" was already formulating in UP's collective mind.

Although never the

original intent, "Dithers" indirectly explained Upper Playground without the founders having to come out and explicitly say exactly what it was that they were doing with the brand. The stories did it for them: Art is a lifestyle, and Upper Playground wanted to be the brand to encapsulate the energy of this vibrant generation.

294
ALBERT REYES

295
ALBERT REYES

296
ALBERT REYES

297
ALBERT REYES

MOVIES EASE THE PAIN
WORKING IN ▬▬▬▬ A MEDIUM
PUSH IT AS MUCH AS YOU CAN
AND TRUST THAT EVERYTHING
THAT HAPPENS HAPPENS FOR A REASON
SHE NEEDS A FRIEND
LIKE I NEED A DENTIST
THIS WORLD IS CORRUPT
SO I'LL JUST GIVE A FUCK

299
ALBERT REYES

300
ALBERT REYES

301
ALBERT REYES

302
ALBERT REYES

ALBERT
REYES

ALBERT
REYES

GIANT
ONE

306
**GIANT
ONE**

307
**GIANT
ONE**

308
**GIANT
ONE**

309
**GIANT
ONE**

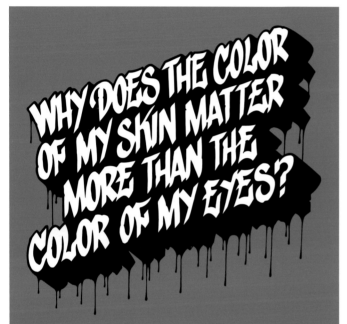

VERITAS · PIETAS · INTEGRITAS

AMOR AETERNUS

313
GIANT
ONE

314
BIGFOOT

315
BIGFOOT

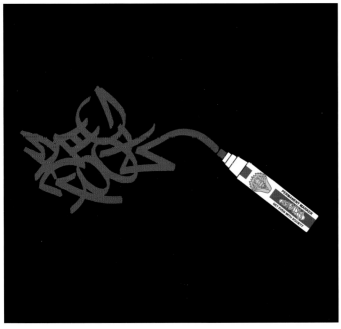

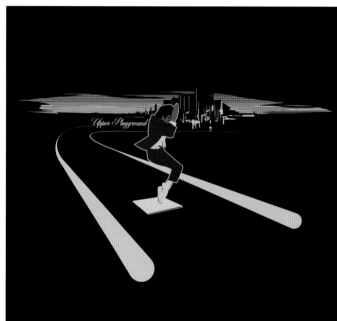

323
DENIS KENNEDY

324
DENIS KENNEDY

325
DENIS KENNEDY

326
DENIS KENNEDY

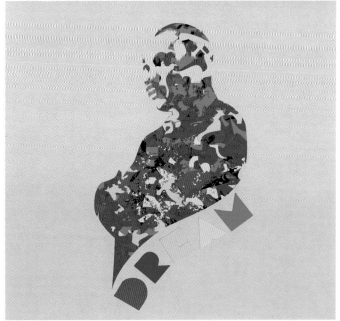

327
DENIS KENNEDY

328
DENIS KENNEDY

329
DENIS KENNEDY

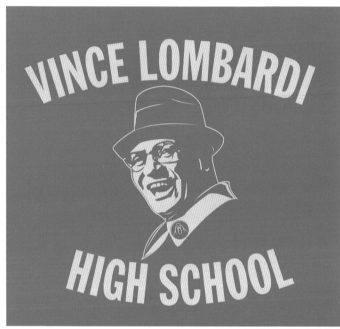

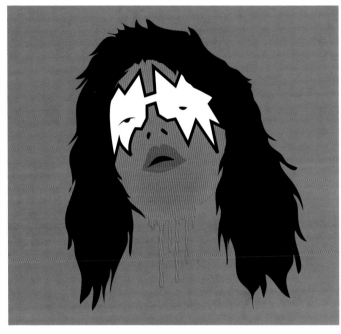

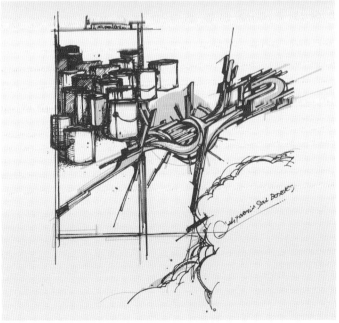

337
GREY

338
GREY

339
GREY

340
GREY

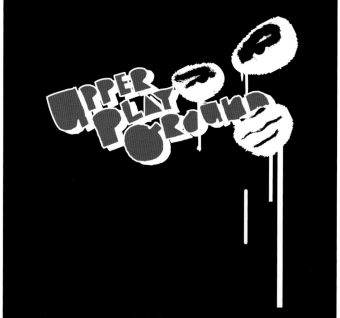

341
GREY

342
GREY

343
GREY

344
EWOK

346
**DORA
DRIMALAS**

347
**DORA
DRIMALAS**

348
**DORA
DRIMALAS**

349
MR. JAGO

350
TASACO
HASU

351
TASACO
HASU

352
KUSTAA
SASKI

353
KUSTAA
SASKI

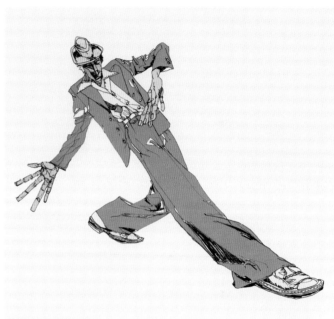

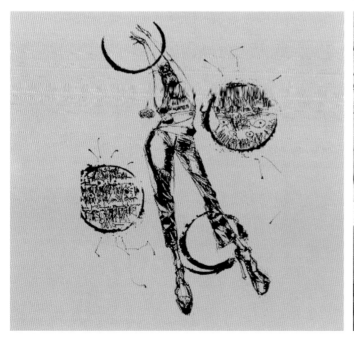

358
RICKY POWELL

359
RICKY POWELL

360
RICKY POWELL

ERIC B. + CHUCK D. CHILLING BACKSTAGE MSG '87

Ricky Powell

JAM MASTER JAY '87

KRS-ONE LIVE NYC '89

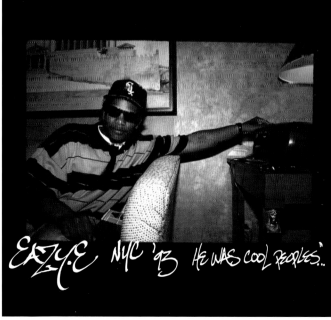

EAZY.E NYC '93 HE WAS COOL PEOPLES..

I remember talking to Matt over the phone in early 2001 (I thought he wore a beret and had the beatnik beard thing going from the way he sounded). He flew me out for a solo show in August 2001 and turned out to be just like me, maybe even more so. A few years later, I came out to San Francisco with "The Dynamic Duo" Zephyr and Dr. Revolt, two of NYC's all-time greatest graff writers/painters (one of their claims to fame is painting the original "Wild Style" logo for the Wild Style movie, and an historic appearance in Style Wars). I forget the show/opening we had at FIFTY24SF Gallery, but I'm sure it was hype. Matt commissioned the two "rebels" to do pieces up over on the roof of UP.

364
RICKY
POWELL

365
RICKY
POWELL

366
RICKY
POWELL

367
RICKY
POWELL

DMC - Hip Hop Agronaut '87

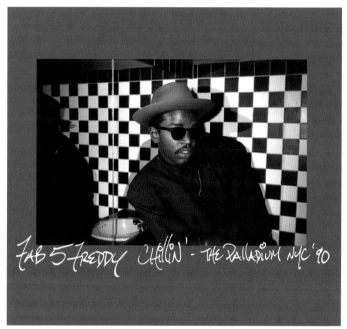

Fab 5 Freddy Chillin' - The Palladium NYC '90

Eric Sermon Chillins w/ KRS-One NYC '88

370
SAM FLORES

371
SAM FLORES

372
SAM FLORES

SAM
FLORES

SAM
FLORES

SAM
FLORES

SAM
FLORES

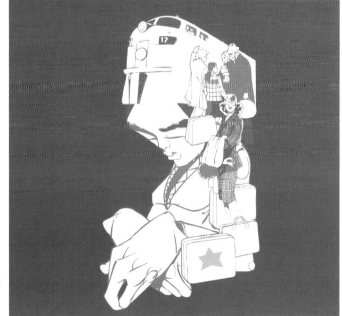

377
SAM FLORES

378
SAM FLORES

379
SAM FLORES

380
SAM FLORES

SAM
FLORES

SAM
FLORES

SAM
FLORES

384
SAM FLORES

385
SAM FLORES

386
SAM FLORES

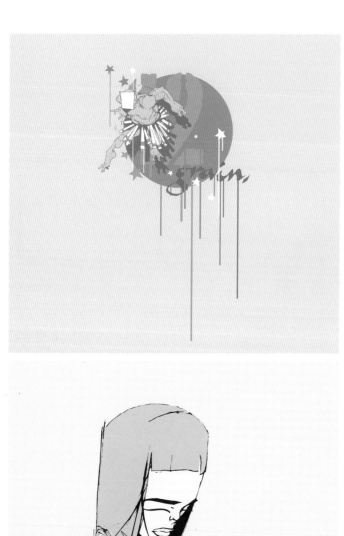

387
SAM FLORES

388
SAM FLORES

389
SAM FLORES

390
SAM FLORES

392
**SAM
FLORES**

393
**DENIS
KENNEDY**

394
**DENIS
KENNEDY**

396
JOHN
DUDA

397
BRAD
DIGITAL

398
BRAD
DIGITAL

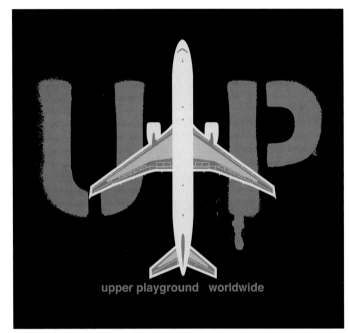

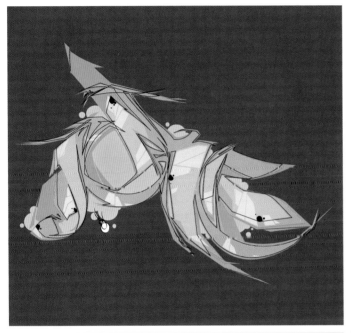

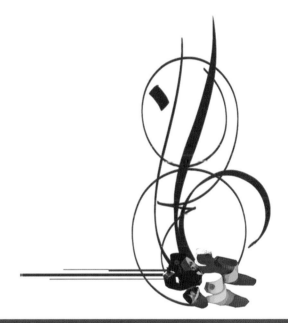

CHRIS
SILVA

LOGAN
HICKS

MORNING
BREATH

When designing the Upper Playground logo as it is now, I tried to simplify the elements down to the simplest that I could, eliminating all the unnecessary frills and make it as clean and readable as possible. Shortly after finishing, UP roped me into an art show tour in Tokyo. After blasting the city with stickers all day and night, Matt and I sat in a second story restaurant looking over Shibuya, where we located a few stickers from the view. I remember him saying, "Now that's a good logo, I can make it out from here." I think UP might have even offered to pay for dinner after that comment, but I wouldn't bet on it.

BRIAN FLYNN

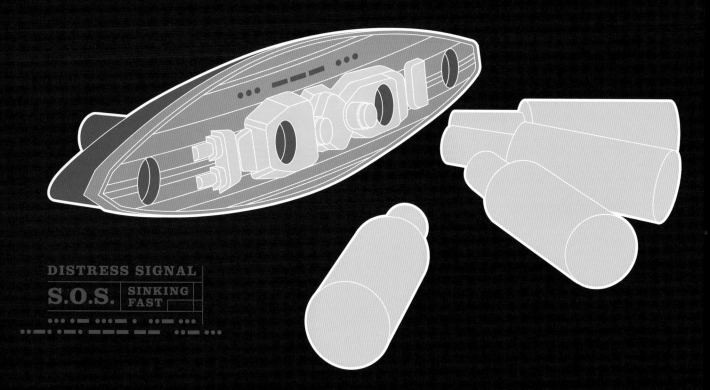

DISTRESS SIGNAL

S.O.S. SINKING
FAST

#11
**BRIAN
FLYNN**

#12
**WILL
BARRAS**

#13
**LONDON
POLICE**

#14
**LONDON
POLICE**

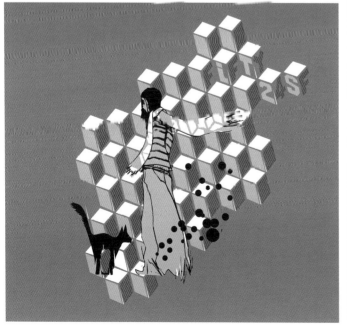

415
DAVE SCHUBERT

416
AIYANA UDESEN

417
AIYANA UDESEN

SHADING TECHNIQUES

CROSS HATCHING IS THE QUICKEST WAY TO MAKE SOMETHING SHADY..

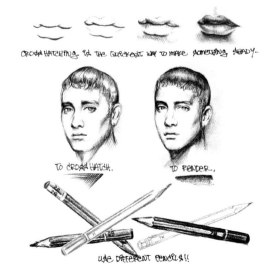

TO CROSS HATCH.   TO RENDER..

USE DIFFERENT PENCILS!!

BRAIDS & CORN ROWS

THE POSSIBILITIES ARE ENDLESS..

COLIN
MILLER

ANDY
MUELLER

ANDY
MUELLER

GALO

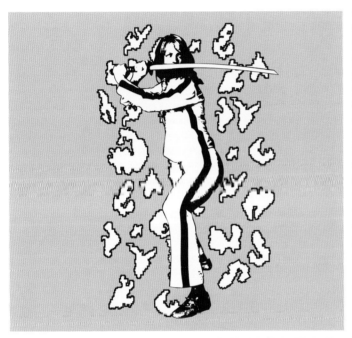

422
**MARK
BODE**

423
**CODY
HUDSON**

424
**CODY
HUDSON**

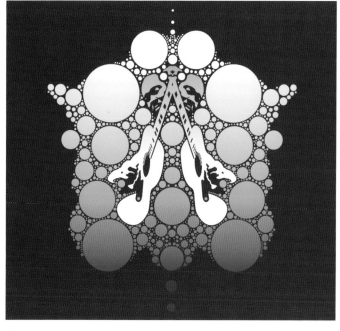

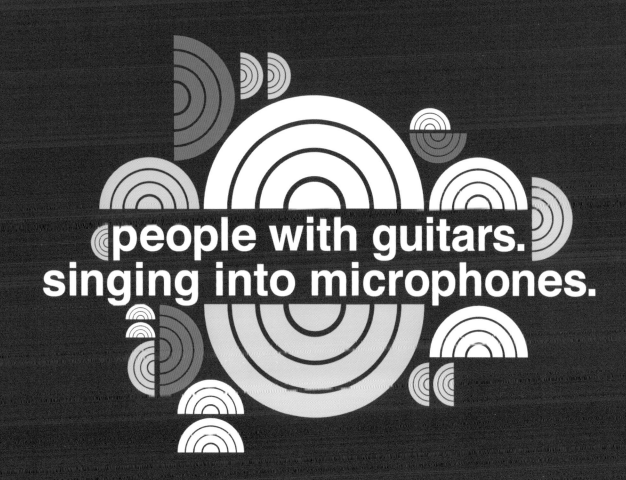

people with guitars.
singing into microphones.

TWØ THØUS AND FIVE

05

JEREMY FISH
ADAM HARTEAU
ANTHONY YANKOVIC
DENIS KENNEDY
BLY FORDHAM
SAM FLORES
N8 VAN DYKE
NOME
RICKY POWELL
DORA DRIMALAS
DAVID CHOE
SLICK
GIANT ONE
HERBERT BAGLIONE   ROB ABEYTA JR.
MENTA   SICKBOY
DAVE SCHUBERT   CYCLE
DAZE   COPE
KARINE LEUNG   GHOST
RICHARD COLMAN   PHASE 2
CYRIL MAZZARD   GREY
MORNING BREATH   CHRIS SILVA
KEGR   REVOLT
CASTLE CPH   FAILE
ALBERT REYES   TOFER
KUSTAA SASKI   EVAQ
ROB MARS   INSECT
URBAN MEDIUM   MARS-1
NAGO   IZ THE WHIZ
MAROK   NATE CRANE
CHRIS PASTRAS   CORO
LONDON POLICE   ELECTRIC HEAT
ANDY MUELLER   FLOYD JACKSON
MR JAGO   GUILLAUME WOLF
ANDY JENKINS
BLADE
DALEK
WILL BARRAS
NO PATTERN

Our tale is now handed over to fine artist and for-ever-wild thing David Choe, who has been a vital part of the Upper Playground tale for nearly a decade. In 2005, a solo show of Mr Choe's at the FIFTY24SF Gallery garnered much attention and accolades for both the artist and brand. The cast of characters involves Ted Shred, Choe, Revelli, and a dungeon of secrets.

On with Mr. Choe's story… "If you smelled my paintings a decade ago, you would catch wafts of waffle cone with traces of orange sherbet laced with mint chocolate chip, because the only place my paintings had ever been shown was in an ice cream shop. I could not catch a break. This is what people call the 'salad days,' except I was eating Top Ramen. Then there was this tiny ad in a magazine for an art gallery in San Francisco, and I said 'fuck it,' made color copies of all my art, and walked in there. At the time I didn't know this, but I would later find out that in the entire history of Up-per Playground, I was the only 'artist' that has ever walked into the gallery with my portfolio and got a show (there's still hope for you dropouts and art fags!). Every artist that has or had been shown at FIFTY24SF was contacted by the gallery itself to exhibit in the space, but not me. And to this I owe the DJ, Ted Shred.

"Matt Revelli, the owner, was in the gallery when I walked in, but he didn't want anything to do with my portfolio, or me, and went downstairs. I didn't know Matt was the main man, so Ted Shred, who was working the register, said that he, Ted, owned Upper Playground and impersonated the 'boss.' Out of sheer boredom, he asked to look at my black book. He was like, 'Oh SHIT! This is really good stuff, can you do my album cover? Hey, I need to show this to Matt!' I said, 'Why are you showing it to Matt? I thought you said you were the main guy in charge?' …Anyway, Ted takes me downstairs to the dungeon basement where the UP secret headquarters used to be, and Matt says, 'What the fuck, Ted? You can't just keep bringing random people down here.' I then showed Matt my book and the rest is history.

"Because of Upper Playground, I've gotten an opportunity to paint with the best artists in the world, all over the world. I've gotten from rock walls in Shibuya to castles in France; I know what a real Kobe steak and Japanese prison food tastes like. I now know what my piss looks like when it dries on cheap Japanese station-ery; I know how to finagle free cable from all hotel rooms, got to see what vaginas look like all over the world, got to mash through ancient temples in the Japanese country-side, and ride scooters and eat stinky cheese in the south of France. I now know I'm not the only fucked-up one and every artist at Upper Playground has far more serious issues than I do, making me feel pretty damn good about myself. I got to see artists such as Galo take every drug on the planet and not sleep for a week, smoke weed while he's in the shower, and still paint all day and night. I've seen Saber become a Spanish superhero and stop a purse snatcher in Barcelona (all while he was tagging) with lightning quick reflexes with the fucking spray can in his hand, and then stomp a wife beater's face in the next night while the dude was beating his woman in the street. I've seen Saber try to drive a van through a bar because the owner was disrespecting us. I found painter Herbert Baglione in São Paulo and, through Upper Playground, was sharing a bed with him a week later in Paris, eating snails and listening to Sepultura, as we tore up the French landscape. I've gotten the chops to paint extremely large murals in really short periods of time, in front of huge crowds, and for all this, in print, I would like to formally apologize for getting arrested in Japan when I was supposed to be painting. And for everything else, I mean, who else gets to paint and cause trouble for a living? The corporations end up sponsoring our lifestyle with free clothes, Sparks, paint, and for all this I want to say thank you to Matt Revelli, who never promises more than he can offer, but always comes through with his word. In a shady fucking art world where everyone gets burned, Matt always made sure the artists got paid first and everyone else came after. And I want to thank Matt and UP for believing in me, when the only other person that gave me a shot just knew about 31 flavors. Ride or die . . ."

JEREMY FISH

JEREMY FISH

ADAM HARTEAU

ANTHONY
YANKOVIC

ANTHONY
YANKOVIC

ANTHONY
YANKOVIC

ANTHONY
YANKOVIC

442
DENIS KENNEDY

443
DENIS KENNEDY

444
DENIS KENNEDY

445
DENIS KENNEDY

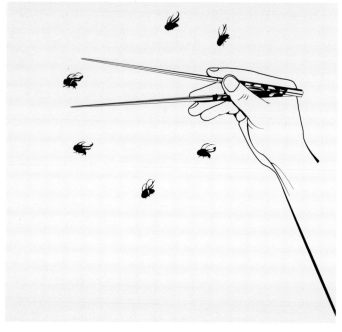

DO THE PEE WEE HERMAN

447
DENIS KENNEDY

448
DENIS KENNEDY

449
DENIS KENNEDY

450
DENIS KENNEDY

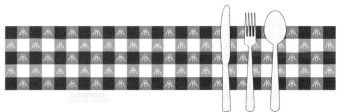

455
DENIS
KENNEDY

456
DENIS
KENNEDY

457
DENIS
KENNEDY

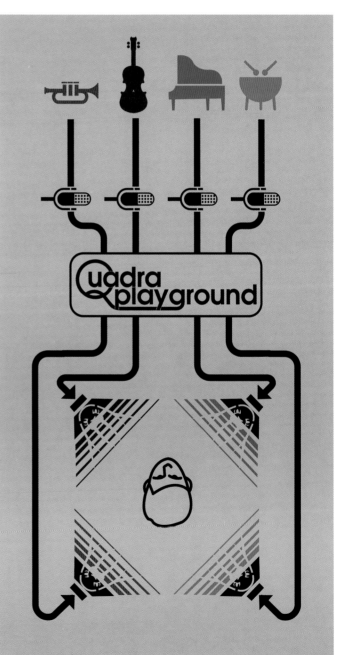

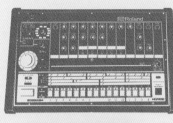
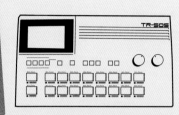

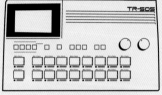

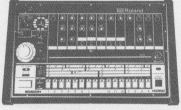
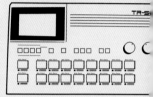

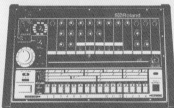
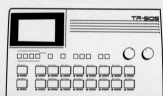
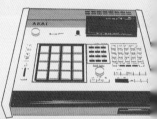
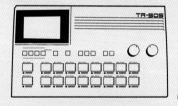

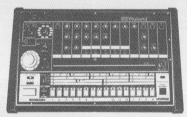
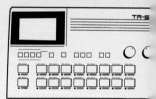

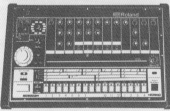
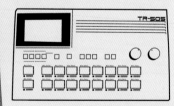

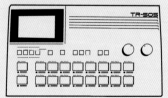

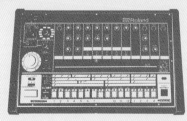
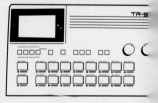

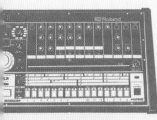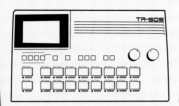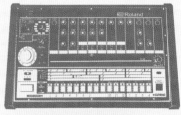
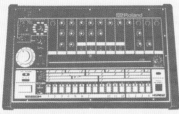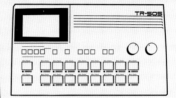
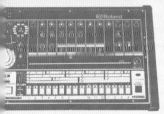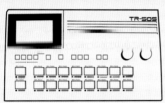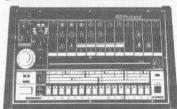
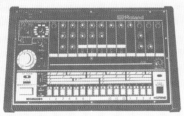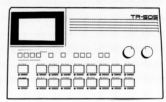
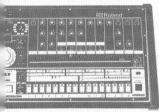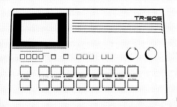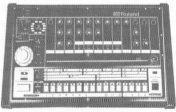
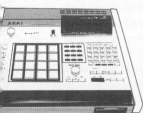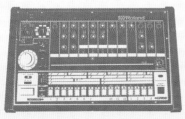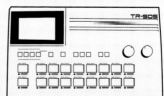

UPPER PLAYGROUND

460
SAM
FLORES

461
SAM
FLORES

462
SAM
FLORES

463
SAM
FLORES

468
SAM FLORES

469
SAM FLORES

470
SAM FLORES

471
SAM FLORES

SAM
FLORES

SAM
FLORES

SAM
FLORES

SAM
FLORES

千本匹

#477

SAM
FLORES

#478

SAM
FLORES

#479

SAM
FLORES

#480

SAM
FLORES

481
SAM
FLORES

482
SAM
FLORES

483
SAM
FLORES

484
SAM
FLORES

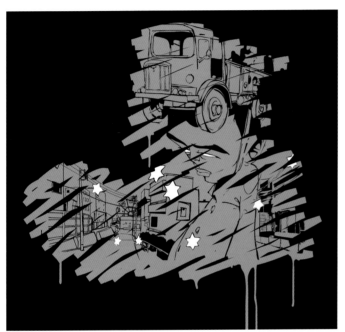

#85
SAM
FLORES

#86
SAM
FLORES

#87
SAM
FLORES

488
SAM FLORES

489
SAM FLORES

490
SAM FLORES

491
SAM FLORES

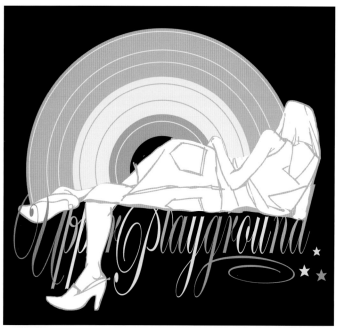

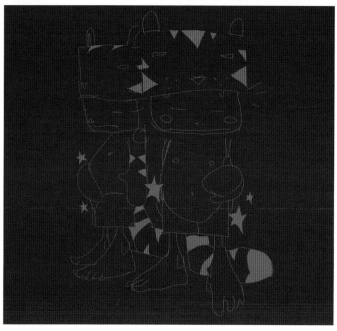

493
DENIS
KENNEDY

494
N8
VAN DYKE

495
NOME

496
NOME

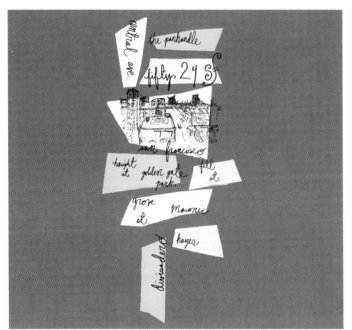

501
RICKY POWELL

502
RICKY POWELL

503
DORA DRIMALAS

504
DORA DRIMALAS

UPPER
PLAYGROUND
SAN FRANCISCO
CALIFORNIA

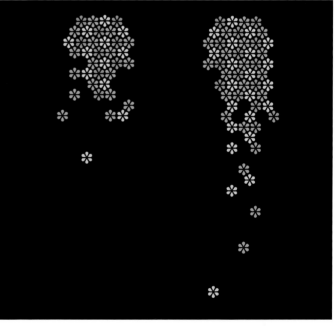

**DORA
DRIMALAS**

**DORA
DRIMALAS**

**DORA
DRIMALAS**

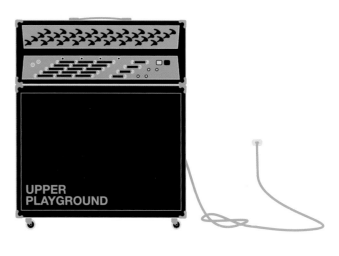

508
DAVID
CHOE

In all my years as an artist I've done things I never thought possible and traveled to places I would have never believed I would ever get to see. **I just never thought it would be with a walrus...**

512
DAVID CHOE

513
DAVID CHOE

514
DAVID CHOE

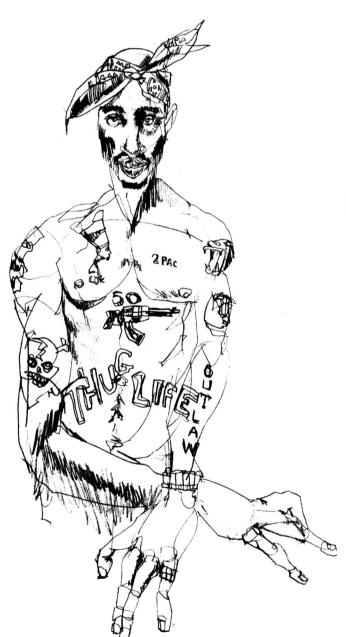

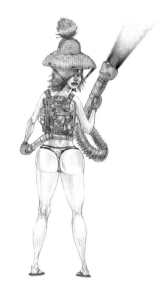

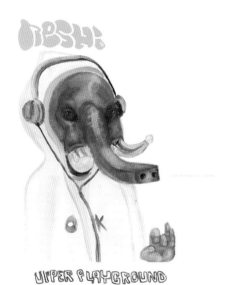

GIANT
ONE

HERBERT
BAGLIONE

HERBERT
BAGLIONE

527
HERBERT BAGLIONE

528
HERBERT BAGLIONE

529
HERBERT BAGLIONE

530
MENTA

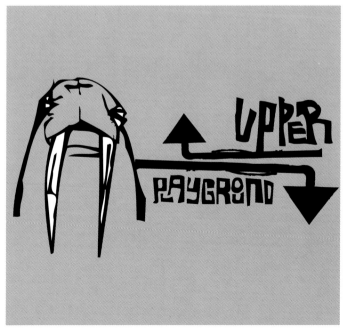

**DAVE
SCHUBERT**

**DAVE
SCHUBERT**

DAZE

DAZE

535
**KARINE
LEUNG**

536
**KARINE
LEUNG**

537
**KARINE
LEUNG**

538
**KARINE
LEUNG**

★ ☆ ☆
MORNING
BREATH

★ ★ ☆
MORNING
BREATH

★ ★ ☆
MORNING
BREATH

★ ★ ☆
BRIAN
FLYNN

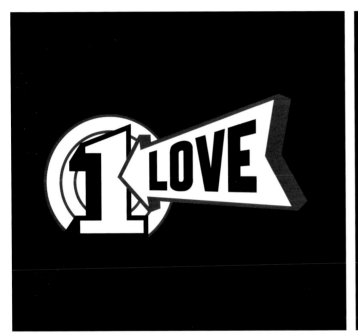

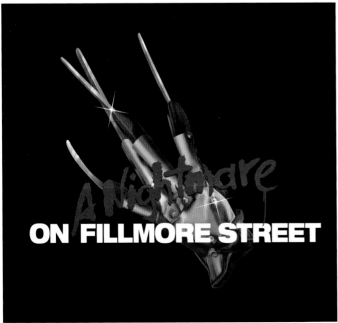

549
ALBERT
REYES

550
CASTLE CPH

551
CASTLE CPH

552
KEGR

554
ANDY MUELLER

555
ANDY MUELLER

556
ANDY MUELLER

557
CODY HUDSON

558
MR. JAGO

559
MR. JAGO

560
ANDY
JENKINS

561
ANDY
JENKINS

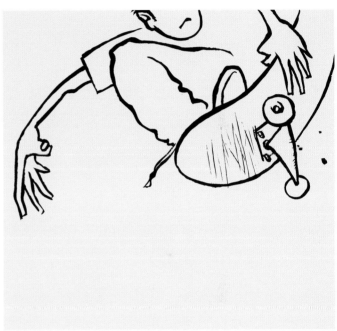

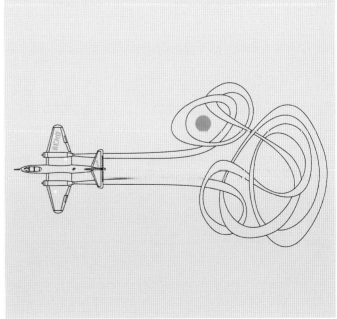

562
BLADE

563
BLADE

564
RICHARD
COLMAN

565
CYRIL
MAZZARD

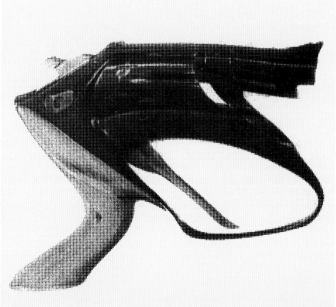

567
WILL BARRAS

568
WILL BARRAS

569
ROB ABEYTA JR.

570
ROB ABEYTA JR.

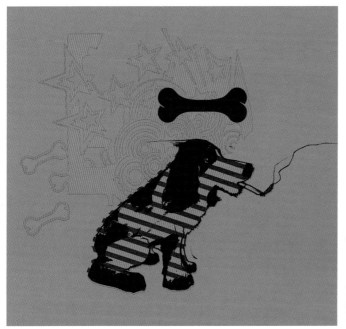

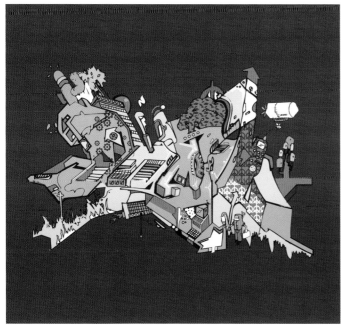

575
COPE

576
GHOST

577
PHASE 2

576
PHASE 2

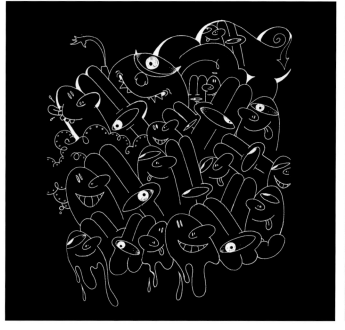

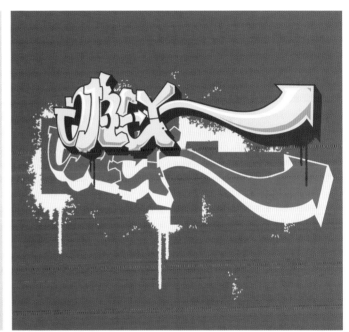

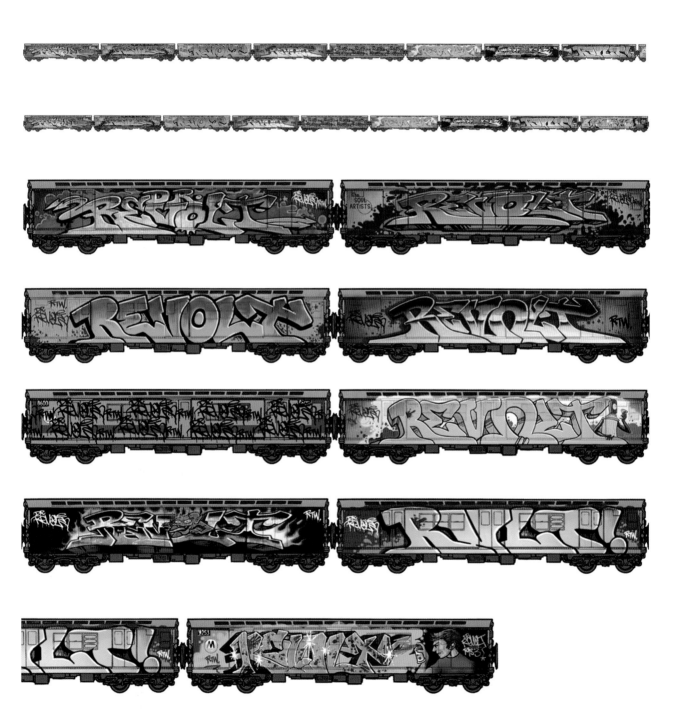

588
ELECTRIC HEAT

589
ELECTRIC HEAT

590
ELECTRIC HEAT

591
FLOYD JACKSON

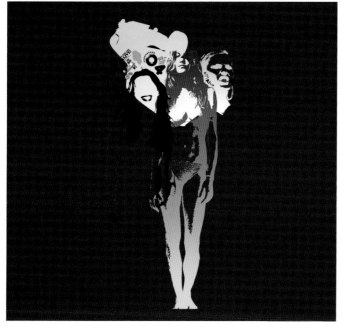

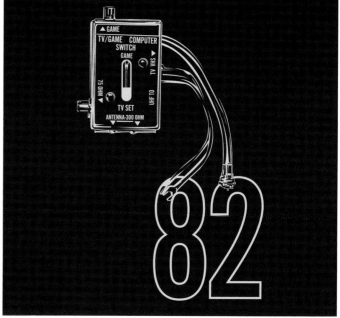

593
NO PATTERN

594
EVAQ

595
**PAUL
INSECT**

596
TOFER

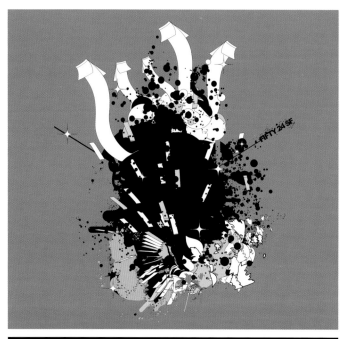

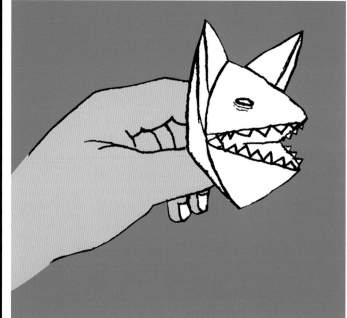

597
MARS-1

598
**NATE
CRANE**

599
IZ THE WIZ

600
CORO

601
CORO

602
CORO

603
CORO

604
CORO

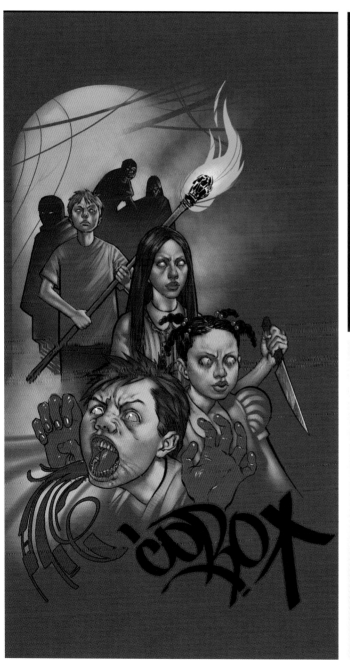

TWØ THØUS AND SIX

06

ESTEVAN ORIOL
EDUARDO RECIFE
SAM FLORES
LONDON POLICE
GROTESK
MAROK
MARS-1
COPE 2
DENIS KENNEDY
RAZA UNO
THOUGHT NINJA
CYCLE
SABER
AARON HORKEY
YOK
DORA DRIMALAS
HERBERT BAGLIONE
JEREMY FISH
GUILLAUME WOLF
DAVID CHOE
ANTHONY YANKOVIC
MORNING BREATH
ALBERT REYES
MASA
UPSO
GREG "CRAOLA" SIMKINS
JORDAN VIRAY
BASCO
DR. LAKRA
VITCHE
ROB ABBYTA JR.

BAST
DAVID LEE
GOREY
GIANT ONE
JR
SEAK
WILL BARRAS
FAILE
PAUL INSECT
BRIAN FLYNN

After great momentum was built during the first half of the decade, Upper Playground had finally got around to the idea of expansion, not just with development within the brand that gave Sam Flores his own line, Twelve Grain, but to expand their retail presence in other cities.

Another theme of UP not mentioned earlier in this text, is the founder's need to out-do himself. That meant consistently more elaborate booths and activities at trade shows, catalogs getting bigger showcasing more than 200 products for each season, pushing the book publishing division, developing housewares, and even beginning a furniture line - all of which

was a logistical nightmare to maintain. Yet it was the mission to get bigger, better, and to think so far outside of the box that nobody could assess or predict the next move. So what would be next in 2006? Opening a new Upper Playground brand exclusive store outside of San Francisco.

The flagship Fillmore store was starting to operate smoothly, and there was plenty of product to fill another store, or multiple stores. Portland happened to be a city where Upper Playground had solid relations and accounts, and it was close enough to San Francisco so they weren't over-extending themselves in terms of distance. The seed was planted

in Portland to open a new retail space, and with the right partners, Upper Playground PDX opened in the fall of 2006. Once a new retail experience was opened and became successful, the owners of UP knew it was possible to open stores themselves as well as with partners who understood the brand.

With Portland, a city relatively unfamiliar with the brand, UP wanted to go big. All of their artists were brought out for the store opening with an exhibition featuring all of their work in a show that would fill the new FIFTY24PDX Gallery space. UP then had the artists painting murals in various locations and at different events around the

city: they brought Z-Trip up to DJ, Estevan Oriol shot Herbert Baglione ads, Sam Flores and Saber painted live, Basco came up from Chile, and there was an event with Aesop Rock and Jeremy Fish signing their Next Best Thing vinyl record collaboration. Portland being somewhat of a smaller city, the atmosphere was that Upper Playground was everywhere; a Walrus invasion, if you will. There was a pre-opening party, the first Thursday event was going off, all the artists were going out every night: If this was going to be the first time UP got to take over another city that was not San Francisco, they had to do it right. What ended up happening was something greater; it became the Upper Playground Olympics.

At one point, amidst the madness, Brazil's Herbert Baglione arrived at the airport and no one thought to pick him up, expecting him to figure it out, armed with only Portuguese and a vivid imagination. Mr. Baglione ended up getting lost for hours in the small Northwestern city. Another set from the Upper Playground playbook: sometimes you are asked to do things on your own, and no matter how ridiculous it may seem for you to be left to your own devices, UP always gives you your freedom, like it or not. Sometimes it doesn't always go as planned, and Mr. Baglione got lost for a good portion of 24 hours only to surface at the store the next day and may or may not still hold a grudge.

The opening of Upper Playground PDX led to the opening of a London retail store in late 2007. The UK customers understood what Upper Playground was all about because of the fact that art translates across cultures, which has proved a benefit to a brand built on the energy of the art world. With "The Run Up" documentary, "UP Until Now" retrospective book, Aesop and Jeremy Fish's collaborative storybook and vinyl single, "Next Best Thing," store expansion, creating the Twelve Grain brand with Sam Flores, and the catalogs growing out of control, 2006 was a year where UP truly upped the ante, even beyond their own expectations. It gave them confidence to know that they could take the brand beyond the typical apparel boundaries, and their customer base would embrace unexpected projects. And of course, everyone at UP happily felt like working 16 hours a day instead of 12.

605
SAM FLORES

606
SAM FLORES

607
SAM FLORES

608
SAM FLORES

608
SAM FLORES

610
SAM FLORES

611
SAM FLORES

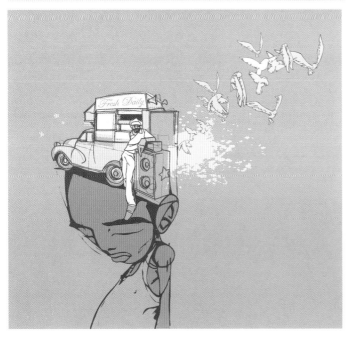

612
SAM FLORES

613
SAM FLORES

614
SAM FLORES

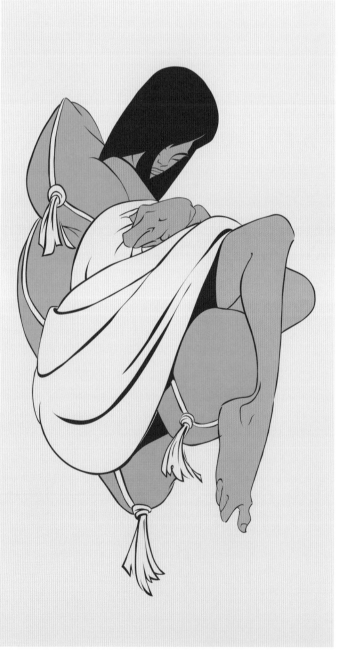

615
SAM
FLORES

616
SAM
FLORES

617
SAM
FLORES

618
SAM
FLORES

621
SAM
FLORES

622
SAM
FLORES

623
SAM
FLORES

624
SAM
FLORES

SAM
FLORES

SAM
FLORES

SAM
FLORES

SAM
FLORES

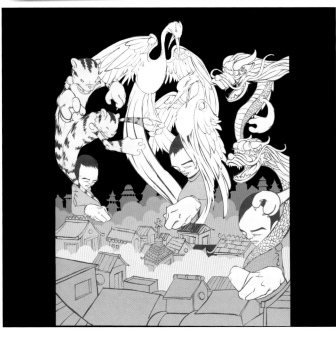

629
SAM FLORES

630
SAM FLORES

631
SAM FLORES

634
**SAM
FLORES**

635
**LONDON
POLICE**

636
**LONDON
POLICE**

ESTEVAN
ORIOL

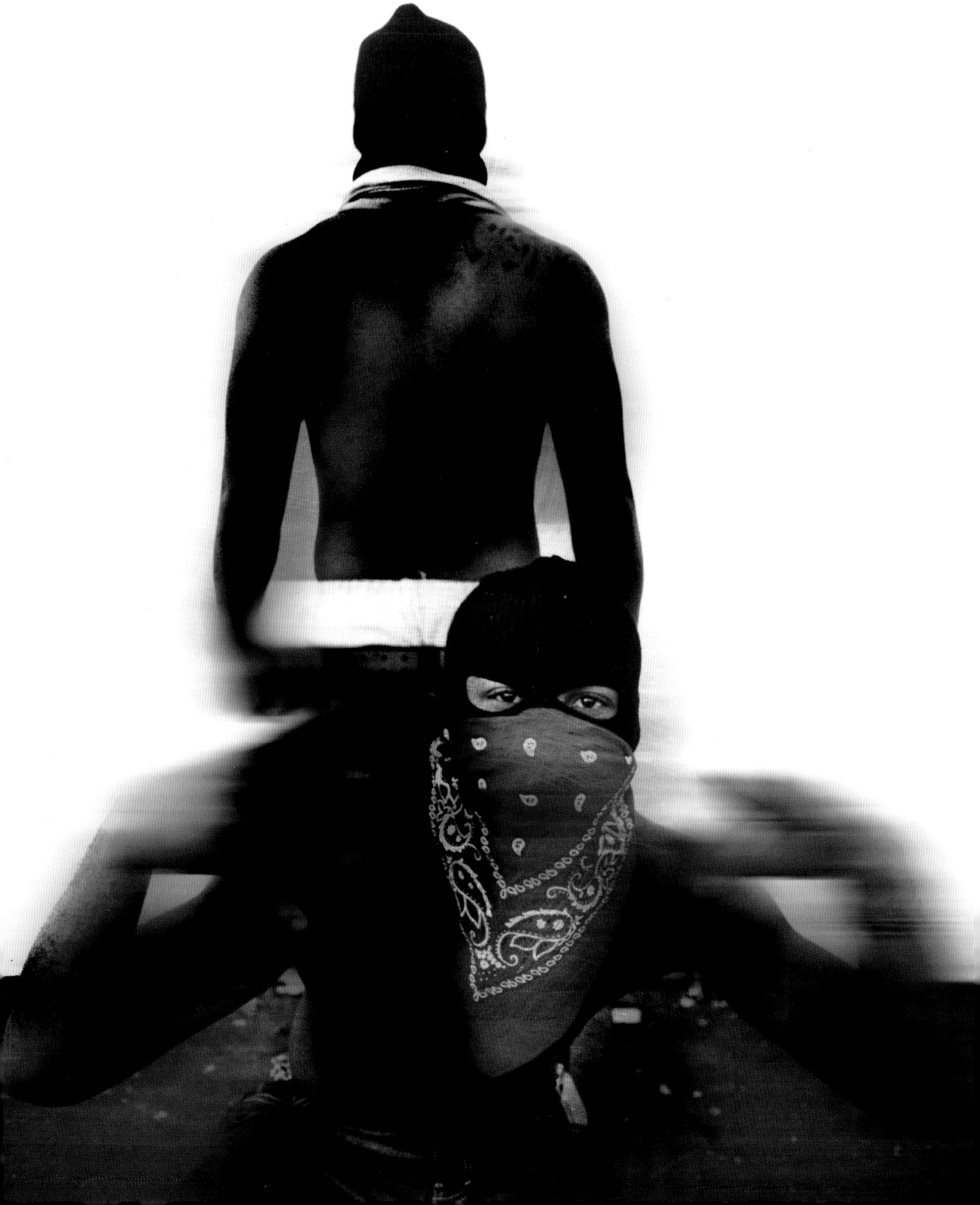

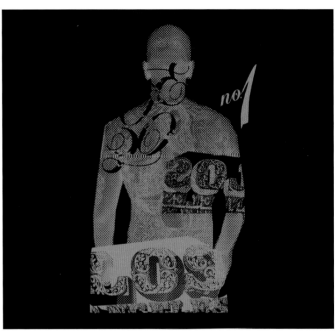

642
**ESTEVAN
ORIOL**

643
**ESTEVAN
ORIOL**

644
**ESTEVAN
ORIOL**

645
**ESTEVAN
ORIOL**

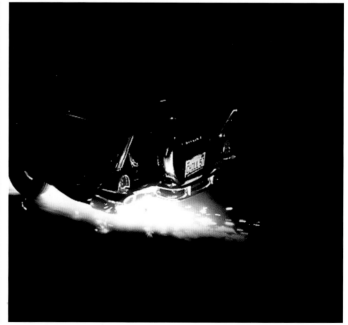

ESTEVAN
ORIOL

ESTEVAN
ORIOL

ESTEVAN
ORIOL

I like the LA Fingers design that I shot a lot, but a lot of people bit that one big time. That shit cracks me up. I also like the one with the wifey holding the shotgun. That is a real crowd pleaser. I just like doing business with Upper Playground because it is straight up no bullshit; there is no other agenda, it is what it is.

649
ESTEVAN ORIOL

650
ESTEVAN ORIOL

651
ESTEVAN ORIOL

652
ESTEVAN ORIOL

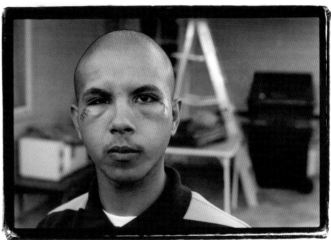

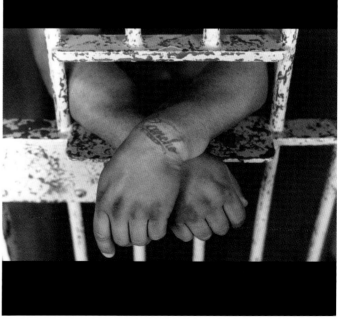

ESTEVAN
ORIOL

ESTEVAN
ORIOL

ESTEVAN
ORIOL

Air Fart 05

UPPER PLAYGROUND
HOUSTON CHAPTER

UPPER PLAYGROUND

EARTH SHAKER

DJ SCREW
R.I.P

UPPER PLAYGROUND

CAN YOU SEE ME?

H SLABS

H SLABS

swang and swerve
from side to side

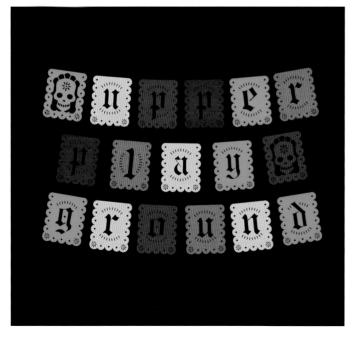

676
THOUGHT NINJA

677
DENIS KENNEDY

678
DENIS KENNEDY

679
DENIS KENNEDY

680
DENIS KENNEDY

681
DENIS KENNEDY

682
DENIS KENNEDY

EL UPPER PLAYGROUND

COSTA OESTE

COSTA ESTE

SAN FRANCISCO

NUEVA YORK

CERVEZAS FRIAS

MUJERES CALIENTES

684
RAZA
UNO

685
RAZA
UNO

686
RAZA
UNO

687
RAZA
UNO

692
GROTESK

693
DENIS
KENNEDY

694
DENIS
KENNEDY

695
DENIS
KENNEDY

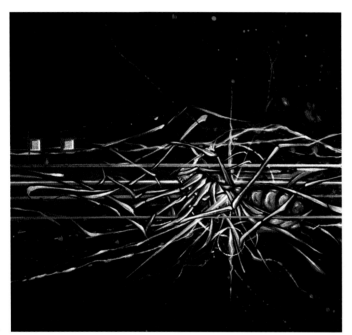

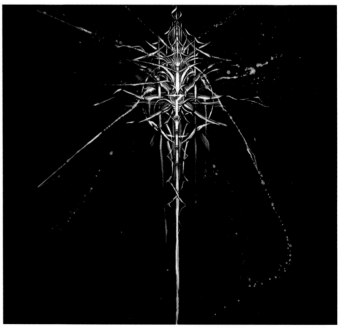

©AHORKEY

HERBERT BAGLIONE

HERBERT BAGLIONE

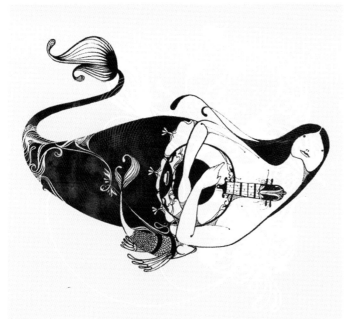

706
HERBERT
BAGLIONE

707
HERBERT
BAGLIONE

708
HERBERT
BAGLIONE

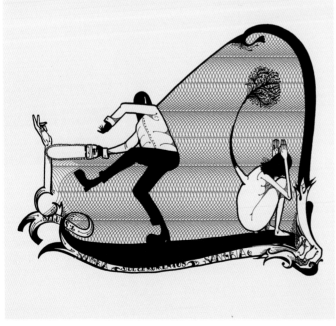

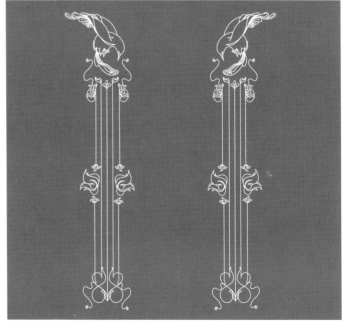

JEREMY
FISH

JEREMY
FISH

JEREMY
FISH

JEREMY
FISH

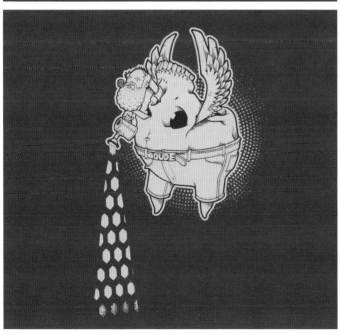

715
JEREMY
FISH

716
JEREMY
FISH

717
JEREMY
FISH

718
JEREMY
FISH

725
JEREMY FISH

726
JEREMY FISH

727
GUILLAUME WOLF

728
GUILLAUME WOLF

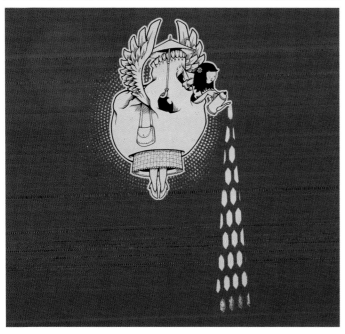

731
DAVID CHOE

732
DAVID CHOE

733
DAVID CHOE

734
DAVID CHOE

FAILE

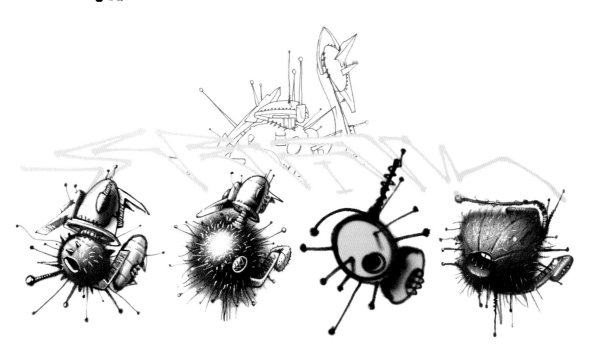

743
MORNING BREATH

744
MORNING BREATH

745
MORNING BREATH

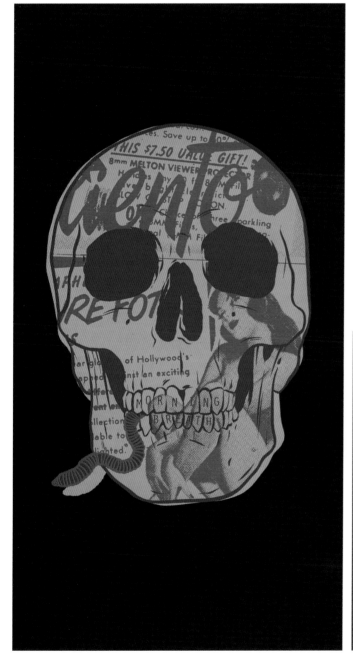

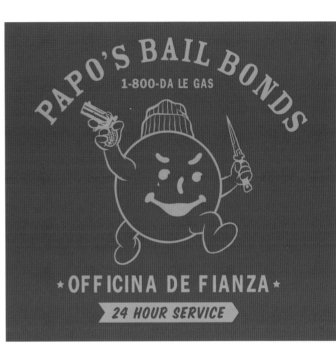

755
CRAOLA

756
CRAOLA

757
CRAOLA

758
CRAOLA

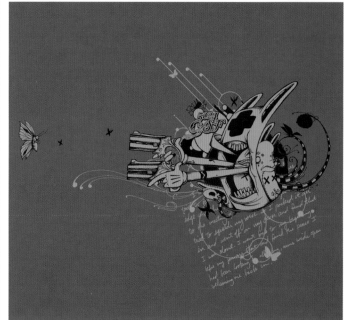

759
CRAOLA

760
CRAOLA

761
JORDAN
VIRAY

762
JORDAN
VIRAY

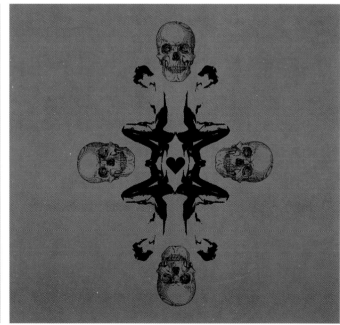

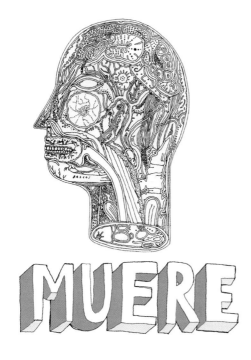

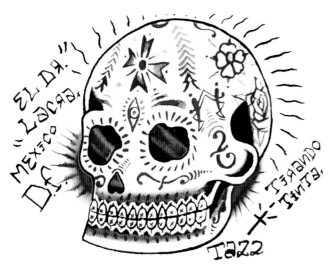

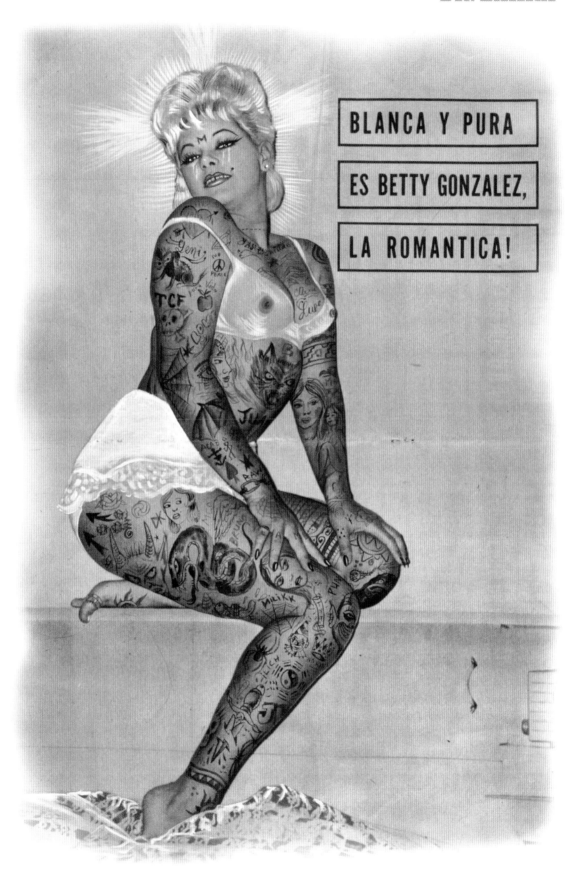

BLANCA Y PURA

ES BETTY GONZALEZ,

LA ROMANTICA!

769

**PAUL
INSECT**

770

**PAUL
INSECT**

771

**ROB
ABEYTA JR.**

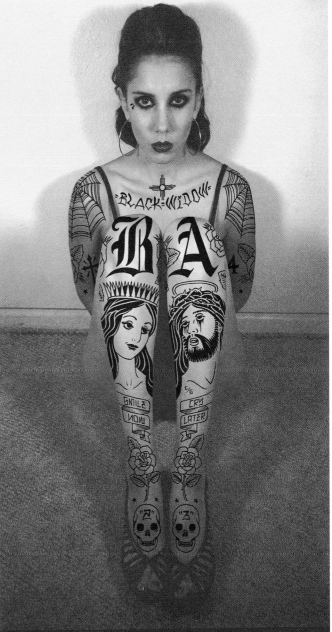

777

**HERBERT
BAGLIONE**

778

**DENIS
KENNEDY**

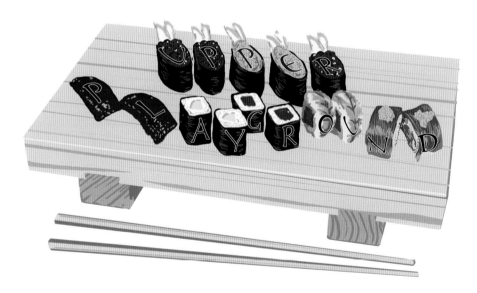

TWØ THØUS AND SEVEN

07

SAM FLORES
REYES
DALEK
MATZU
DENIS KENNEDY
THOUGHT NINJA
CODY HUDSON
GROTESK
DORA DRIMALAS
DATE FARMERS   JB
MAYA HAYUK   RAZA UNO
JEREMY FISH   MUNK ONE
BEN TOUR   DAVID CHOE
RETNA   CODY HUDSON
GEORGE CAMPISE   DALEK
HENRY LEWIS   USUGROW
SARA SNOW   ANTHONY YANKOVIC
ROB ABEYTA JR.   STOHEAD
DAVE ELLIS   CHRISTIAN ACKER
HERBERT BAGLIONE   BLAINE FONTANA
PETE PANCIERA   MEAR ONE
ALEX PARDEE   GIANT ONE
TABAS   RICKY POWELL
MARCO CIBOLA   ALËX ONE
MAROK   CHUEY
BASCO   MORNING BREATH
SABER   NUNCA
ESTEVAN ORIOL   PATRICK MARTINEZ
INSECT   JASON TYLER GRACE
BOOGIE   VITCHE
GREG "CRAOLA" SIMKINS

Jeremy Fish, a long-term member of the UP family, who is currently designing his own Super-Fishal line through UP, was asked about the history of his relationship with the brand. The San Francisco North Beach ambassador had an interesting take, and unexpected sports analogy: "It's funny, I'm not much for team sports. I was never much of a 'joiner' as a kid; clubs and after school groups were for nerds. For the last ten years or so, Upper Playground is one of the only 'teams' in my life that I was more than proud to be on the roster. Our team has been able to travel the world, fill galleries, produce books and films, and yes, make thousands of T- shirts that hopefully made people's lives better. The personalities behind the Walrus are visionaries in a sea of naysayers and purists. Our team leads movements, as opposed to the followers and some bandwagoners of today's oversaturated art circus. I hope to someday be in the yearbook next to some of the most relevant contemporary visual artists of our time, people who I am proud to call coaches and teammates on a team that won't be easily forgotten in the legacy that is this goofy art world."

Somehow, some way, Jeremy Fish was able to weasel his way into almost four straight group shows UP hosted earlier at FIF-TY24SF Gallery (though he probably won't admit to it). And UP waited until 2007 to finally give him his own line, SuperFishal, perhaps as punishment, after about four or five years of steady collaboration. But it's hard in this day and age to think of Fish not being part of the UP family, especially because, like Elle MacPherson to the cover of the SI swimsuit edition, JFish has the most gallery shows to date, as well as having created countless popular graphics, and he embodies the essence of the San Francisco personality that UP stands for.

Because UP has never done anything on a scale within their means, adding SuperFishal just wasn't enough; the beginning of 2007 saw another move of the offices, this time from 252 Fillmore Street over to a 6,500 square foot warehouse in the Dog-patch neighborhood of San Francisco. That quickly increased again less than a year later to two spaces totaling 13,000 square feet in total. It seemed ridiculous, albeit necessary, because it allowed UP to change how they operated as a brand; more space for inventory, a real headquarters to stage ads, develop product, build catalogs, shoot products, get the business end of things together, as well as play basketball, write on the walls, play indoor soccer, skateboard, and get the operation running efficiently without having to step over someone's computer on the way to the bathroom.

If you want to roll out a store, a fine-looking retail establishment, where you build the displays, create a gallery space, and have all of your woodwork looking sharp when you only have six weeks to get it all together, who are you going to call? The UP furniture designer, Francisco Robles (along with his co-worker, Miguel). This pair has been the backbone of UP expansion. If you think your day is busy, then get a glimpse of a typical Francisco day when working on UP time: Wake-up at 5AM in Fairfield, California (approximately 45 miles from San Francisco) on a Saturday, drive over an hour-and-a-half to SF, finish building out a trade-show booth by 6PM, get in a van, drive all night to Las Vegas, arrive at 9AM, set up the entire booth, and then maybe catch some shuteye.

Or better yet, "Hey Francisco, we need you to design the Upper Playground Los Angeles store in eight weeks, and it's understood you have a full-time job as an accomplished woodworker, so you can only do the LA store on nights and weekends, basically working 40 hours a week at night on top of the 40+ you do for your real job. Is that cool?" No problem. Bottom line, some people think they work hard, but Francisco barely sleeps, works seven days a week, does incredible work, and never complains. That is Francisco Robles.

But his story is not only about building retail spaces. In January 2007, FIFTY24SF Gallery exhibited a special show featuring Francisco's collaborations in furniture design with many of UP's top artistic talent. The show featured a Herbert Baglione dining set, Tiffany Bozic bed set, Sam Flores sake bar, Jeremy Fish couch and turtle table, David Choe chair, Basco table, and Saber dresser, among others. The artists' vision, along with Francisco's woodworking expertise, allowed for the UP Furniture line to spring to life. Features in Juxtapoz Art & Culture Magazine followed, as well as many collectors and connoisseurs of the fine arts becoming interested in the experimental aspect of creating high-end, artist-designed home furniture. Somewhere, a David Choe painted, Francisco-created hallway chair is being used to simply read the Sunday New York Times.

780
**SAM
FLORES**

781
**SAM
FLORES**

782
**SAM
FLORES**

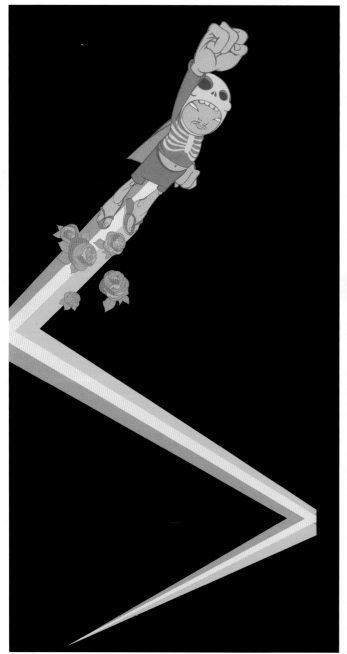

784
SAM FLORES

785
SAM FLORES

786
SAM FLORES

SAM
FLORES

SAM
FLORES

SAM
FLORES

SAM
FLORES

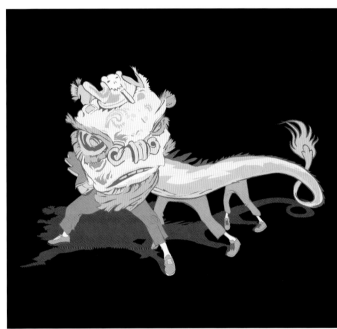

791
SAM
FLORES

792
SAM
FLORES

793
SAM
FLORES

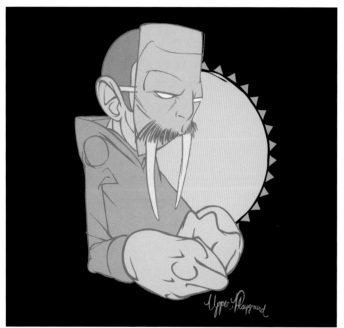

794
SAM
FLORES

795
SAM
FLORES

796
SAM
FLORES

797
SAM
FLORES

798
SAM
FLORES

799
SAM
FLORES

800
SAM
FLORES

801
SAM
FLORES

803
MATZU

804
MATZU

805
MATZU

806
DENIS
KENNEDY

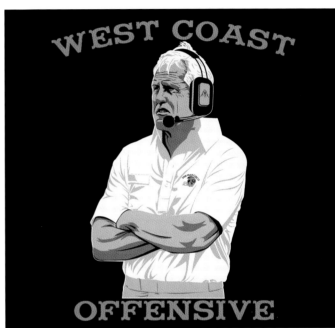

811
DENIS KENNEDY

812
DENIS KENNEDY

813
DENIS KENNEDY

814
DENIS KENNEDY

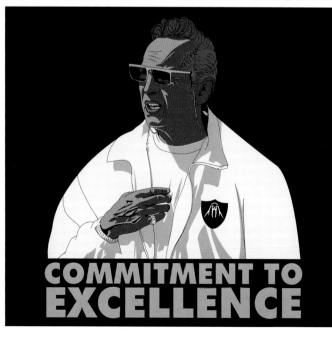

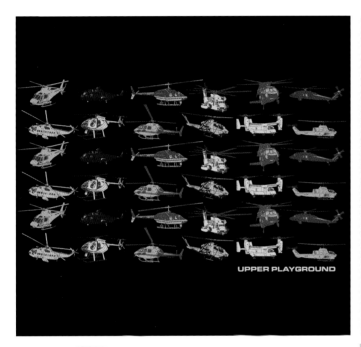

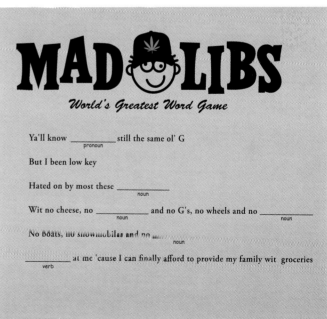

819
DENIS
KENNEDY

820
DENIS
KENNEDY

821
DENIS
KENNEDY

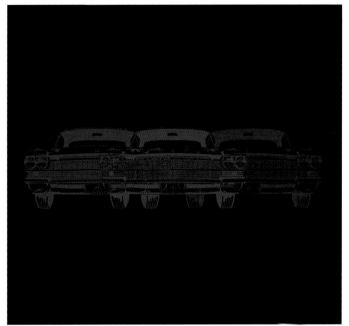

DORA
DRIMALAS

DORA
DRIMALAS

DORA
DRIMALAS

DATE
FARMERS

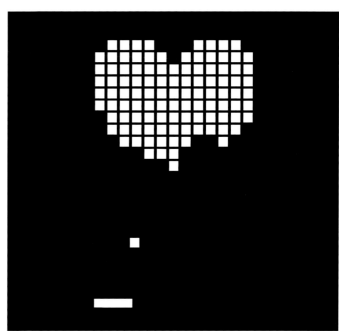

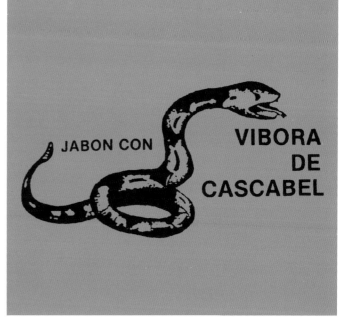

831
GROTESK

832
GROTESK

833
GROTESK

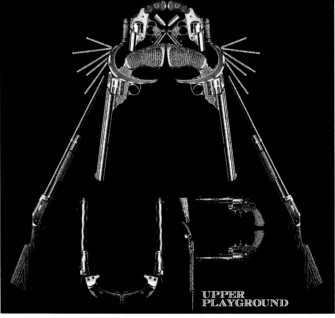

SUPER CHANGO

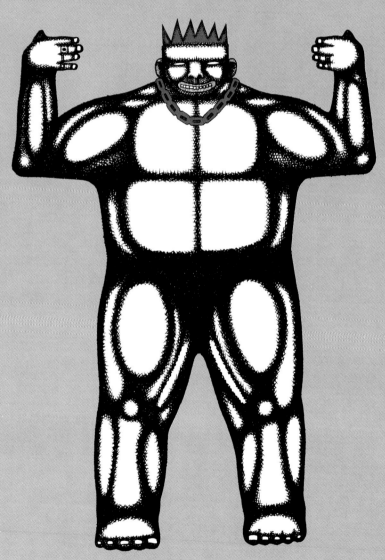

839
DATE
FARMERS

840
DATE
FARMERS

841
DATE
FARMERS

842
DATE
FARMERS

845
JEREMY FISH

846
JEREMY FISH

847
JEREMY FISH

848
JEREMY FISH

849
JEREMY FISH

850
JEREMY FISH

851
JEREMY FISH

852
JEREMY FISH

853
JEREMY
FISH

854
JEREMY
FISH

855
JEREMY
FISH

856
JEREMY
FISH

JEREMY
FISH

JEREMY
FISH

JEREMY
FISH

JEREMY
FISH

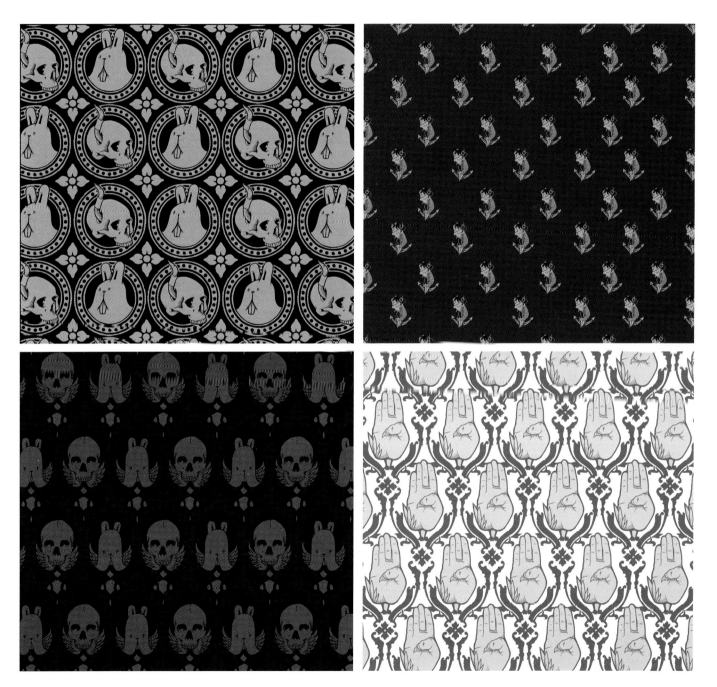

866
JEREMY FISH

867
JEREMY FISH

868
JEREMY FISH

869
JEREMY FISH

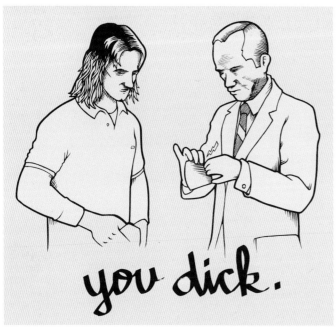

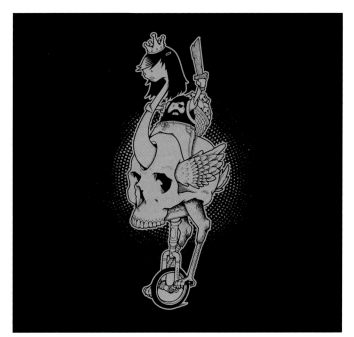

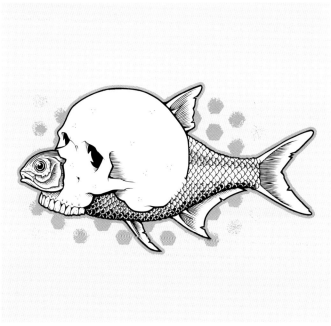

882
RETNA

883
RETNA

884
GEORGE CAMPISE

885
HENRY LEWIS

386
**ROB
ABEYTA JR**

387
**ROB
ABEYTA JR.**

388
**SARA
SNOW**

389
**DAVID
ELLIS**

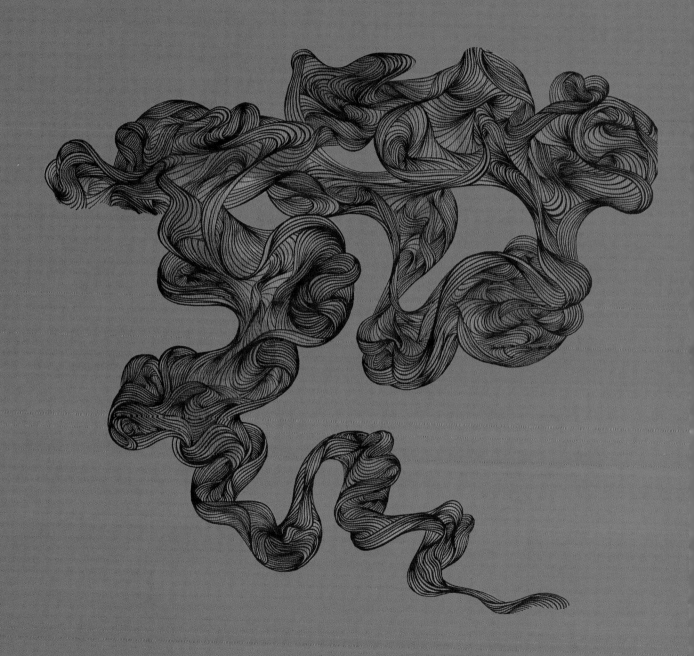

892
HERBERT
BAGLIONE

893
HERBERT
BAGLIONE

894
HERBERT
BAGLIONE

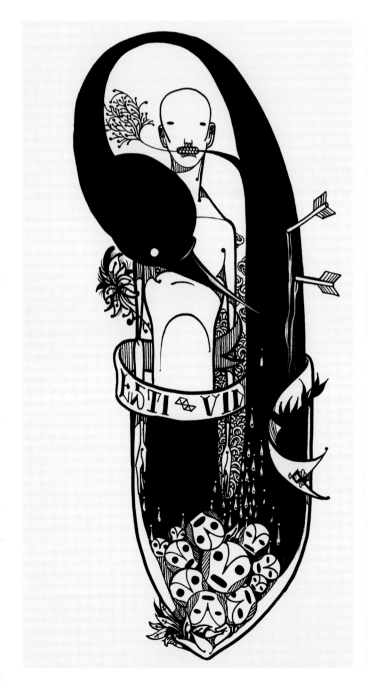

898
HERBERT
BAGLIONE

899
HERBERT
BAGLIONE

900
HERBERT
BAGLIONE

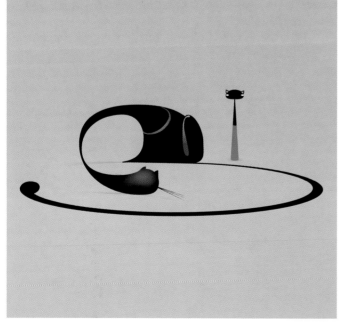

901
HERBERT BAGLIONE

902
HERBERT BAGLIONE

903
BASCO

904
PETE PANCIERA

Every once in a while UP will toss some ideas at me and want to see me take them on, which can be interesting. My interpretation can go in some really weird direction, or just a basic bold rendering. One time in particular, we talked about doing a take on Full Metal Jacket, where the guy eats a shotgun blast, and I WANTED to do this crazy bloody huge horrifying graphic, but I was kind of scared of putting in the time and then having it get rejected, so I played it safe and turned in a graphic that was rather tame. Then UP called and said "What if you went crazier and made it more aggressive and violent?" That's when I realized that we're on the same page and it comforted me. So I made a way more fucked up version of it.

905
ALEX PARDEE

906
ALEX PARDEE

907
ALEX PARDEE

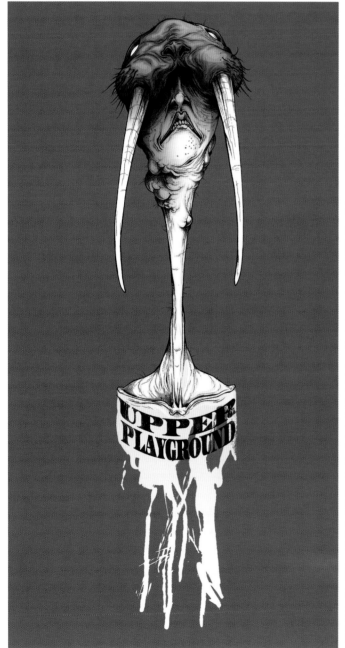

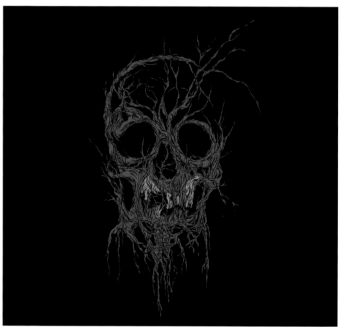

308
ALEX PARDEE

309
ALEX PARDEE

310
ALEX PARDEE

311
ALEX PARDEE

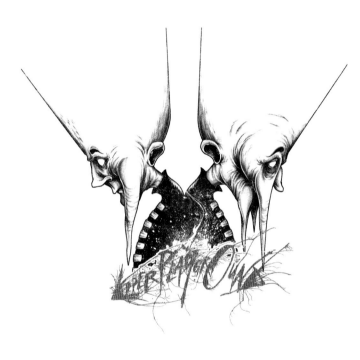

912
ALEX
PARDEE

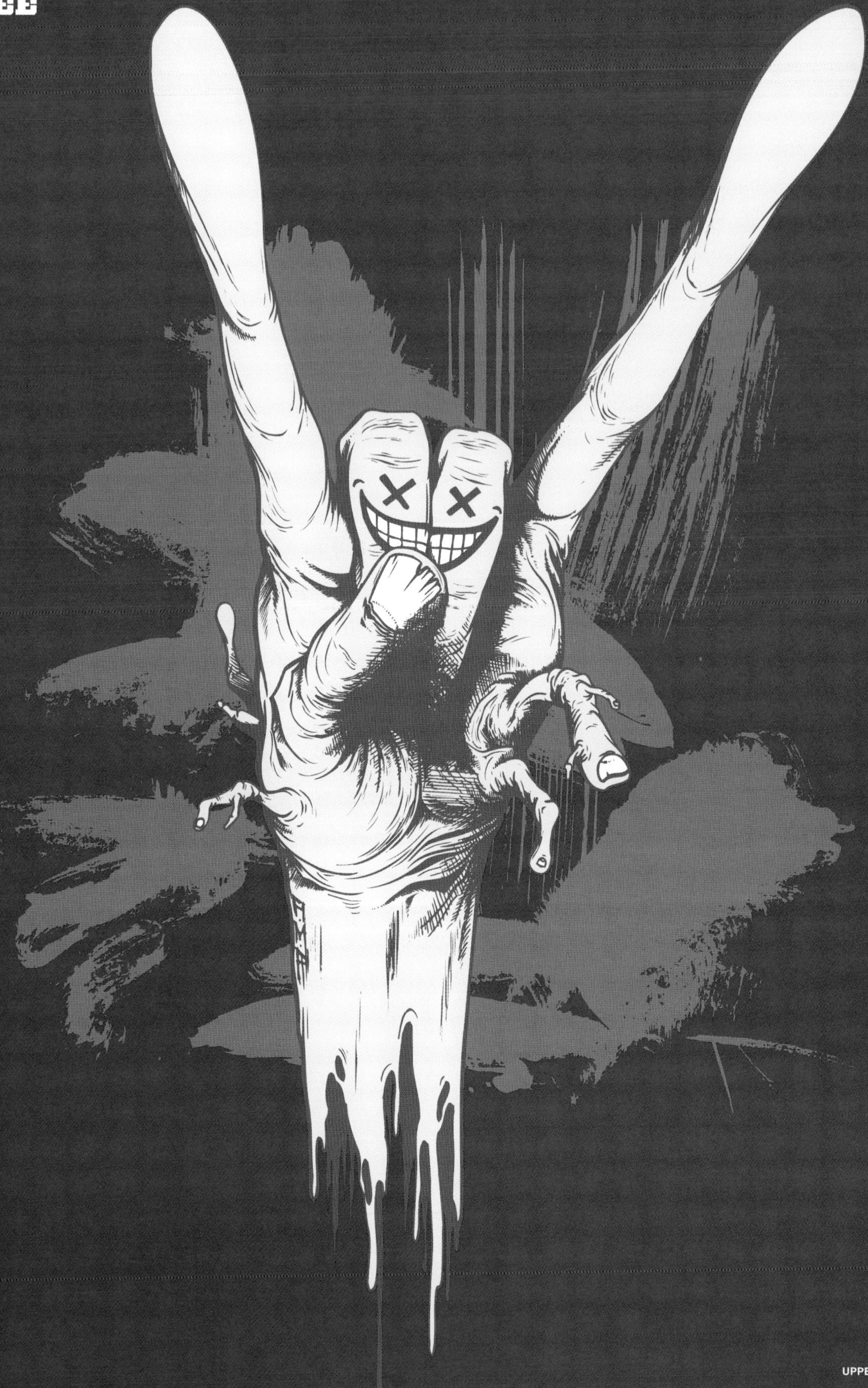

UPPER PLAYGROUND

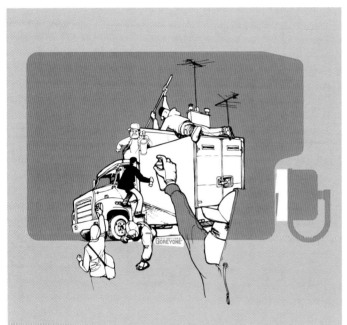

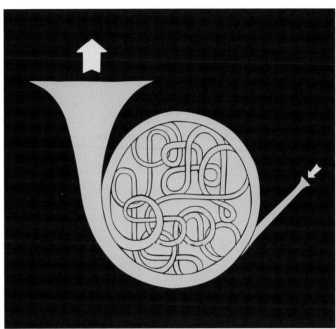

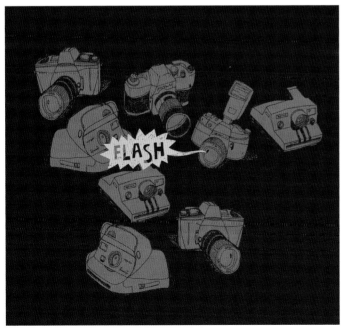

917
SABER

918
SABER

919
SABER

924
ESTEVAN ORIOL

925
ESTEVAN ORIOL

926
ESTEVAN ORIOL

927
ESTEVAN ORIOL

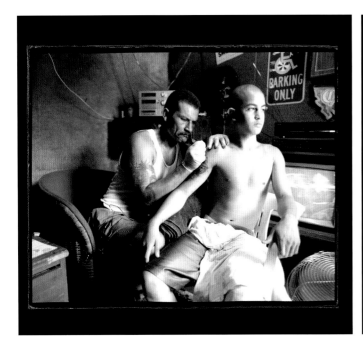

931
ESTEVAN
ORIOL

932
ESTEVAN
ORIOL

933
ESTEVAN
ORIOL

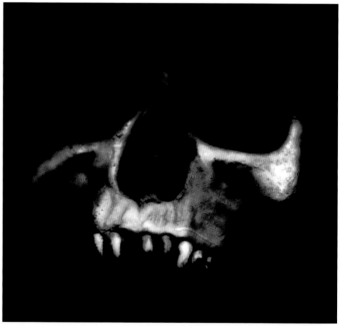

935
ESTEVAN
ORIOL

936
ESTEVAN
ORIOL

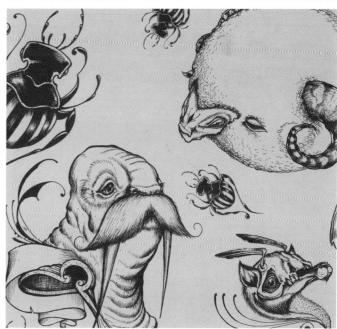

944
RAZA
UNO

945
RAZA
UNO

946
MUNK
ONE

947
MUNK
ONE

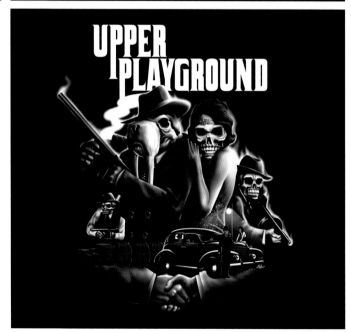

948
REYES

949
DALEK

950
THOUGHT
NINJA

951
THOUGHT
NINJA

954
USUGROW

955
**ANTHONY
YANKOVIC**

956
STOHEAD

957
ADNAUSEUM

**BLAINE
FONTANA**
    **BLAINE
FONTANA**
    MEAR ONE
    MEAR ONE

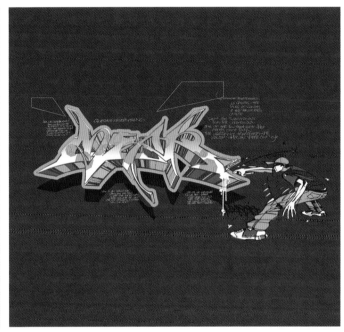

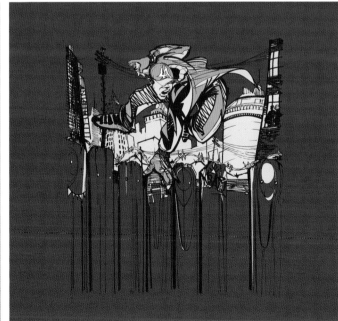

963
RICKY POWELL

964
ALËX ONE

965
CHUEY

966
MORNING BREATH

967
NUNCA

968
NUNCA

969
NUNCA

970
NUNCA

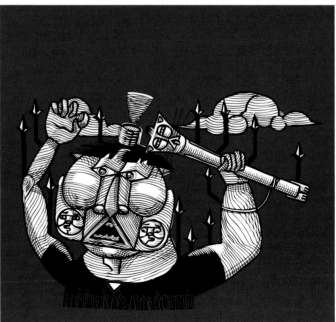

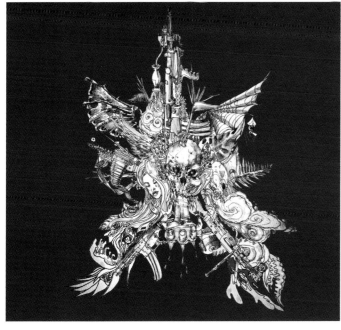

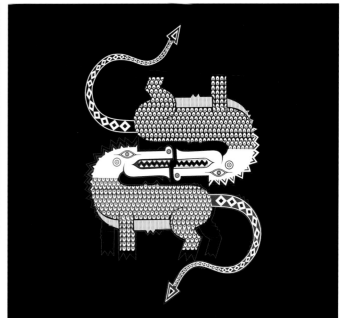

977
AJR

978
PATRICK
MARTINEZ

979
CRAOLA

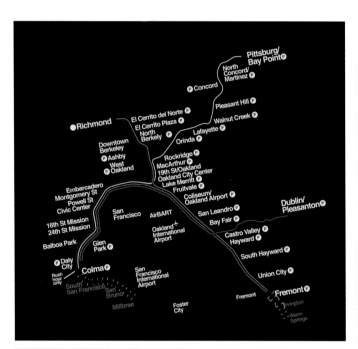

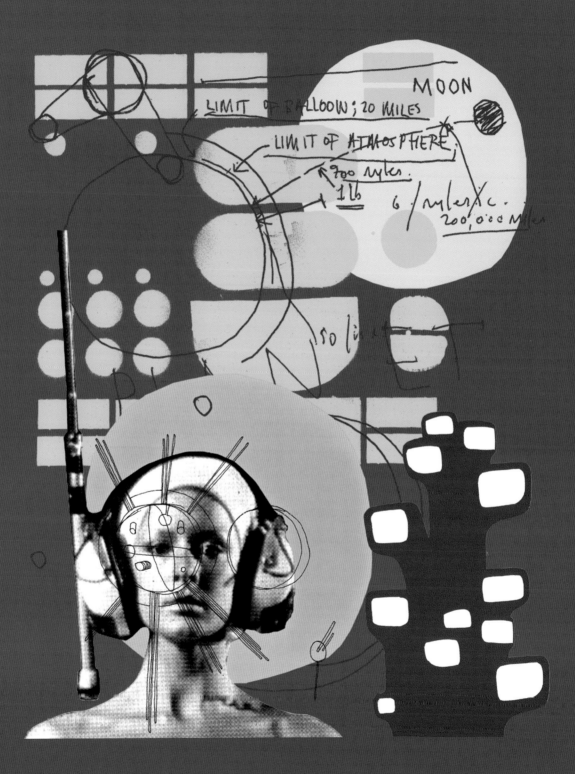

TWØ THØUS AND EIGHT

08

ALEX PARDEE
DATE FARMERS
EDUARDO RECIFE
DORA DRIMALAS
ANDY MUELLER
VITCHE
JEREMY FISH
REGINO GONZALES
GROTESK
ARMSROCK
SAM FLORES
DENIS KENNEDY
KORALIE
ESTEVAN ORIOL
CUM*
MORNING BREATH
MICHAEL SIEBEN
MICKEY DUZYJ
DAVID CHOE
CHUEY
USUGROW
MUNK ONE
BEN TOUR
SAELEE OH
GUILLAUME WOLF
AUGOR
OBLVN
GREG "CRAOLA" SIMKINS
BOOGIE
HORT
KENYON BAJUS
NISH
SABER
HANNAH STOUFFER
DAVID ELLIS
REZEON S. DELARGE
EINE
PATRICK MARTINEZ

IDEALIST
VISION LAB
CHRIS LEE
MARCO ZAMORA
N8 VAN DYKE
BASCO
THOUGHT NINJA
DAN CUENCA
RETNA
RINZEN
HYDRO 74
MARIO WAGNER

South Africa became the one location for the aesthetic planning of a unique retail experience in downtown Los Angeles. At the beginning of 2008, LA-based street photographer Estevan Oriol, perhaps one of the most iconic photographers of his generation, flew to Johannesburg, South Africa along with Revelli. There, they discussed the coming openings of both the Upper Playground Los Angeles retail store as well as The Last Laugh, the retail store from Mr. Oriol and his SA Studios' partner, Mister Cartoon. These would become a cluster of stores existing side-by-side in the Skid Row area of downtown LA.

In a hotel previously held-up at gunpoint by Nigerian drug lords, nearby a pool overlooking a zoo with grazing giraffes and elephants, and while suspect cuisine was delivered by a 4-star hotel waiter, Revelli and Mr Oriol planned the necessary steps to complete the construction of what would be four retail stores (UPLA, two Last Laugh spaces, and one "pop-up" establishment for special collaborations) on Skid Row. When the two finally were able to discover the PF Chang's of Johannesburg, exceptional food and discussion followed, and both returned to California refreshed and ready to complete the stores by the middle of 2008.

Estevan Oriol's relationship with Upper Playground has been one of the most dedicated in the brand's history. In numerous shows at FIFTY24SF Gallery, and the establishment of the Estevan Oriol line for UP, Estevan's raw Southern California street culture and celebrity photographs have been vital to UP's evolution in the previous years. The two created an organic type synthesis of UP's artistic reputation in Northern California with the help of Mr. Oriol's strong Southern California aesthetic. As Mr Oriol puts it, "My first connection with Upper Playground was in 2004. They must have emailed me. After a couple art shows at FIFTY24SF Gallery, and being in "The Run Up" documentary, I have worked with them ever since. I've seen how UP and I have similar ways of thinking in our business and personal lives. They are men of their words, so I figured if I was going to do a tee shirt line outside of my Joker Brand, why not do it with someone who is NOT a piece of shit, a thief, and a fucking liar? So I decided to do it with UP. And here we are today, five seasons later, still doing it, kicking ass with stores in Downtown Los Angeles. I like the way it has gone; we just crept into the game without the obvious 'we're here' method."

The year would also find another major collaborative project to which Upper Playground would devote much of their time and energy. The inspiration of this project was then presidential hopeful, Barack Obama. As the company wrote at the time, "On March 4th, 2008, Barack Obama has the chance to secure the

Democratic Party nomination for President by winning the delegates in both Texas and Ohio. We at Upper Playground are pleased to announce our support of Barack Obama in 2008. For too long we have been plagued by mediocrity and incompetence at the Executive level. As an international company, we feel that it is time to support a candidate that truly embodies the American spirit in both his campaign and his ideologies. We believe that Barack Obama is that candidate."

Upper Playground, along with a major roster of artists including the Date Farmers, Alex Pardee, David Choe, Morning Breath, Mac, Grotesk, Ron English, Mear One, and Sam Flores, created limited quantity of signed screenprints to help raise awareness and support that would independently campaign for Obama 2008. The project also included printing T-shirts and hooded sweatshirts of the iconic Shepard Fairey Obama images seen across the world.

The efforts to support Barack Obama created strong media coverage from various outlets, but coverage was not the reason UP would create such a collaborative project with this roster of international artists; it was another instance when the belief that something larger than the brand was occurring, something that made the creative community proud, that exemplified the creative lifestyle that UP had served for a decade. Like "Dithers" and "The Run Up" before it, the energy the creative culture was generating around Obama was a moment in time that UP wanted to be a part of, and contributed to by working with the artists to tell the story of history in the making.

From South Africa, downtown Los Angeles, Barack Obama, another store expansion in Seattle, Washington, the creation of their online magazine, The Citrus Report, and a shoe collaboration with adidas Originals, Upper Playground in 2008 expanded once again. With sights set on Mexico City, Stockholm, Manchester, England, and New York City at the end of year, the UP machine continued to run full steam ahead.

983
ALEX PARDEE

984
ALEX PARDEE

985
ALEX PARDEE

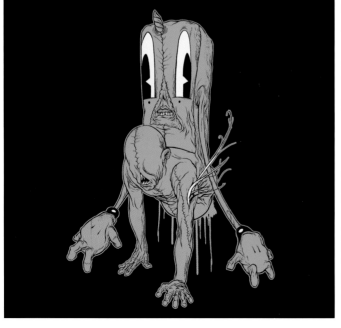

DATE
FARMERS

DATE
FARMERS

DATE
FARMERS

DATE
FARMERS

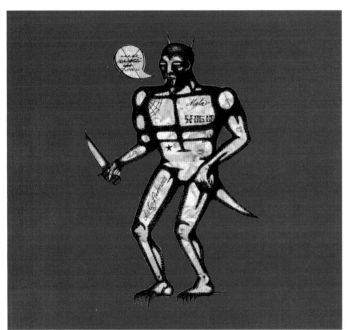

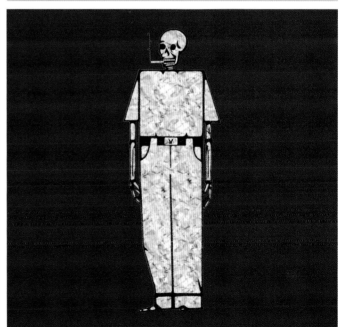

992
DATE FARMERS

993
DATE FARMERS

994
EDUARDO RECIFE

995
EDUARDO RECIFE

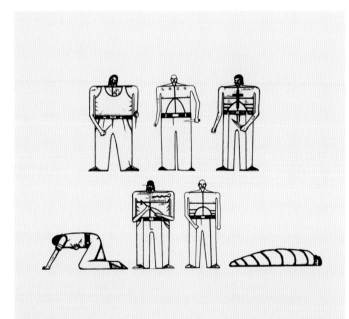

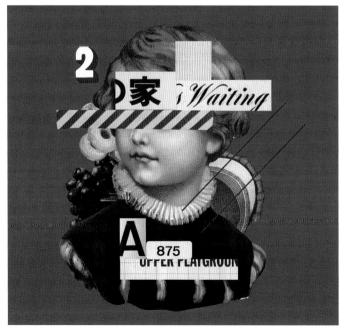

1005
JEREMY FISH

1006
JEREMY FISH

1007
JEREMY FISH

1008
JEREMY FISH

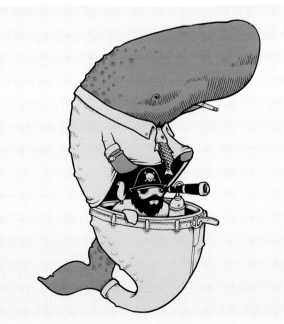

1013
JEREMY FISH

1014
JEREMY FISH

1015
JEREMY FISH

1016
JEREMY FISH

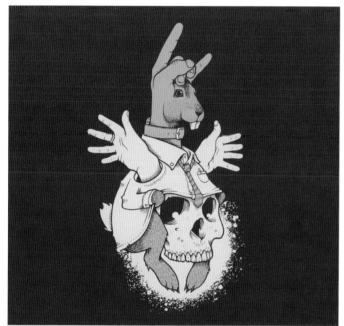

1018
**JEREMY
FISH**

1019
**JEREMY
FISH**

1020
**JEREMY
FISH**

1021
**JEREMY
FISH**

1022
JEREMY FISH

1023
JEREMY FISH

1024
JEREMY FISH

1025
JEREMY FISH

1027
**REGINO
GONZALES**

1028
GROTESK

1029
ARMSROCK

Sometimes I didn't know that certain designs that I did for Upper Playground were going into production. One time one of my graphics, the skull butterfly, was woven into a repeat pattern on a sweater. It looked great. The only problem was other graphics that weren't mine were woven into the sweater as well. Mainly handguns. So, not being a huge fan of guns, the NRA, or people messing with my artwork, I asked UP not to put the sweater into production. Unfortunately, it was too late and the run was finished. So seeing my extremely rare opportunity to have UP in debt to me, I quickly declared that the Upper Playground vs. Hybrid Design Unsportsmanship Challenge was on. After beating UP in bowling, I'm still waiting for the rematch. UP keeps trying to get us to go to archery, but I'm still holding out for bowling.

DORA
DRIMALAS

1030
DORA DRIMALAS

1031
DORA DRIMALAS

1032
DORA DRIMALAS

1033
DORA DRIMALAS

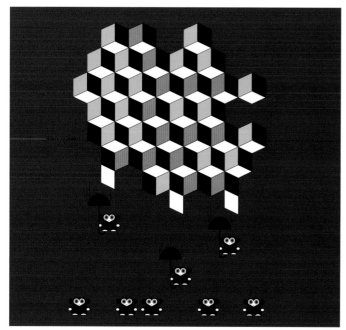

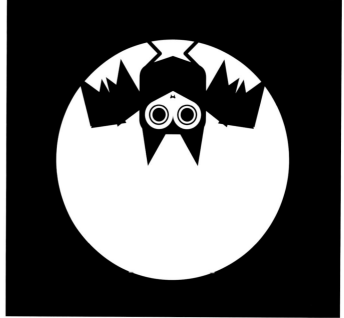

1034
DORA DRIMALAS

1035
DORA DRIMALAS

1036
ANDY MUELLER

1037
VITCHE

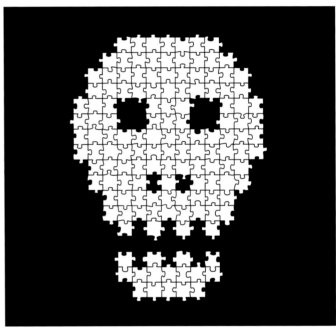

1038
SAM
FLORES

1039
SAM
FLORES

1040
SAM
FLORES

1041
SAM
FLORES

1042
SAM FLORES

1043
SAM FLORES

1044
SAM FLORES

1045
SAM FLORES

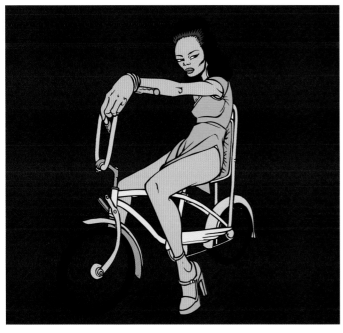

1046
SAM FLORES

1047
SAM FLORES

1048
SAM FLORES

1049
SAM FLORES

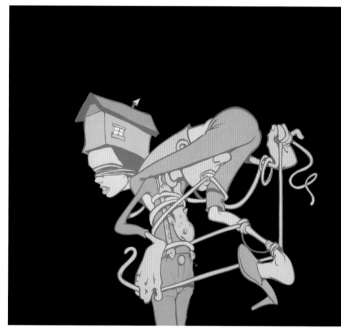

1051
SAM FLORES

1052
SAM FLORES

1053
SAM FLORES

1054
SAM FLORES

SAM
FLORES

SAM
FLORES

SAM
FLORES

SAM
FLORES

1061
SAM FLORES

1062
SAM FLORES

1063
SAM FLORES

1064
DENIS KENNEDY

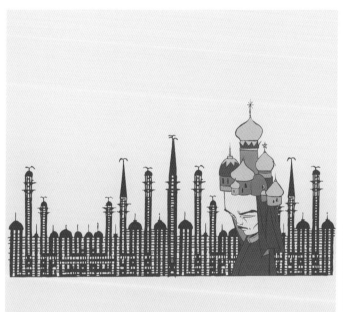

1065
DENIS
KENNEDY

1066
DENIS
KENNEDY

1067
DENIS
KENNEDY

1068
DENIS
KENNEDY

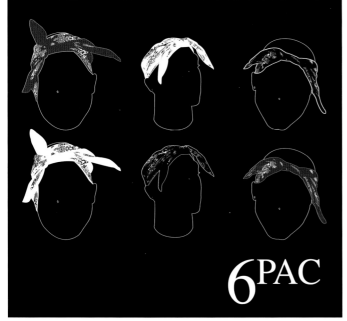

6PAC

DC
Denplex
LEAD FREE
QUICK DRY
spray paint
CAP MATCHES COLOR OF CONTENTS

plasti-kote®
FAST DRY SPRAY PAINT
No. T - 53 SHAMROCK GREEN

PLAYGROUND RED
utilac
spray enamel
5
Benjamin Moore CO.

Color jet
STOPS RUST
spray finishes

Quick 'n Easy
ENAMEL

plasti-kote®
FAST DRY SPRAY PAINT
No. T-4 GLOSS WHITE

sparvar
SPRAY PAINT
QUICK DRY ENAMEL
LIGHT GREEN
No. 5-141

DU PONT
Lucite
SPRAY ENAMEL
FIGHTS RUST

AUTO PRIMER
RUST-OLEUM
STOPS RUST!

1070
DENIS
KENNEDY

1071
DENIS
KENNEDY

1072
DENIS
KENNEDY

1073
DENIS
KENNEDY

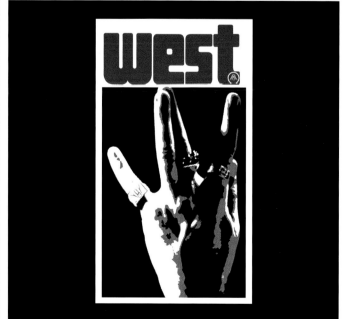

1074
DENIS KENNEDY

1075
DENIS KENNEDY

1076
DENIS KENNEDY

1077
DENIS KENNEDY

DENIS
KENNEDY

DENIS
KENNEDY

DENIS
KENNEDY

1988
CRAOLA

1989
CRAOLA

1990
CRAOLA

Many years ago, a tattooist friend of mine, Jeffrey Page, asked me to do a painting of the walrus and the carpenter for his girl-friend. I started the drawings in my sketchbook but the two had broken up. Fast-forward to the day I was installing my piece in the two-man show at FIFTY24SF. The curator came across the walrus in my sketchbook and wanted me to create it as a shirt design. When I went home I sent the design. Later, I got a frustrated phone call from UP shortly after asking if I took the classes necessary to graduate the second grade. I had spelled "Playground" wrong, and it had already been made into the ad. I was able to fix it for the shirt design, and now I always check my spelling for these things.

GREG "CRAOLA"
SIMKINS

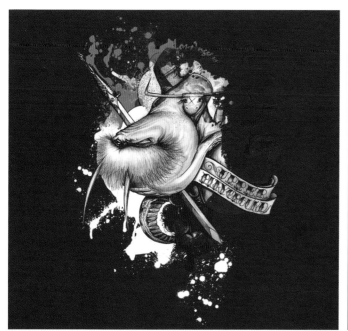

1097
NISH

1098
HORT

1099
KENYON
BAJUS

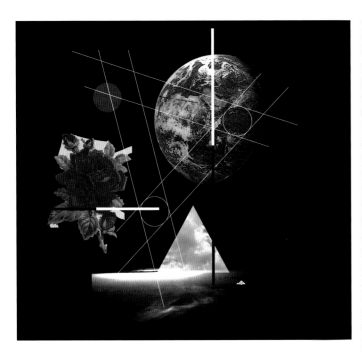

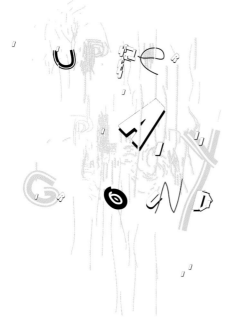

1100
DENIS KENNEDY

1101
KORALIE

1102
KORALIE

1103
KORALIE

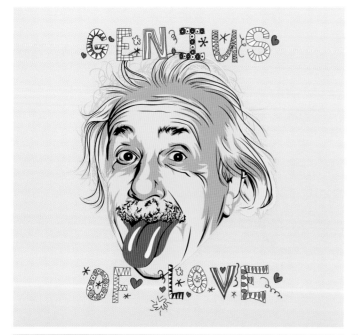

1104
KORALIE

1105
KORALIE

1106
KORALIE

1107
KORALIE

1108
ESTEVAN
ORIOL

1109
ESTEVAN
ORIOL

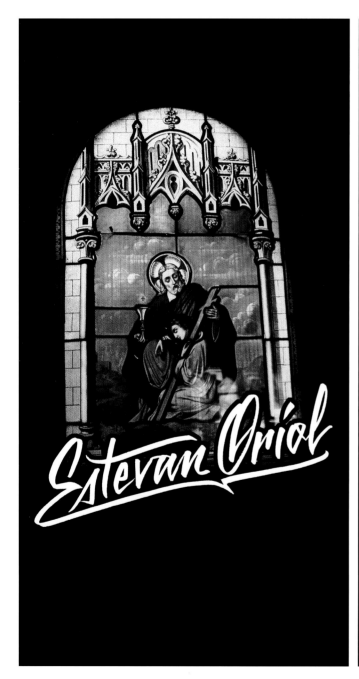

1110
ESTEVAN ORIOL

1111
ESTEVAN ORIOL

1112
ESTEVAN ORIOL

1113
ESTEVAN ORIOL

1119
ESTEVAN
ORIOL

1120
ESTEVAN
ORIOL

1121
ESTEVAN
ORIOL

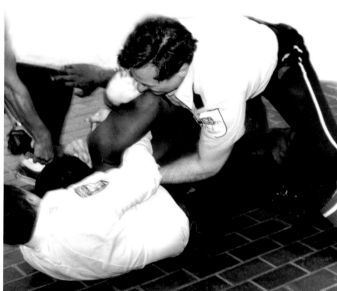

1123
ESTEVAN ORIOL

1124
ESTEVAN ORIOL

1125
ESTEVAN ORIOL

1128
MORNING
BREATH

1129
MORNING
BREATH

1130
MORNING
BREATH

1131
MORNING
BREATH

1132
MORNING BREATH

1133
MORNING BREATH

1134
MORNING BREATH

1135
MORNING BREATH

1136
MORNING BREATH

1137
MORNING BREATH

1138
MORNING BREATH

1139
MORNING BREATH

1143
MORNING BREATH

1144
MORNING BREATH

1145
MICHAEL SIEBEN

PLYWOOD
LIFESTYLE

1147
MICHAEL SIEBEN

1148
VISION LAB

1149
MICKEY DUZYJ

#150
MICKEY DUZYJ

#151
MICKEY DUZYJ

#152
MICKEY DUZYJ

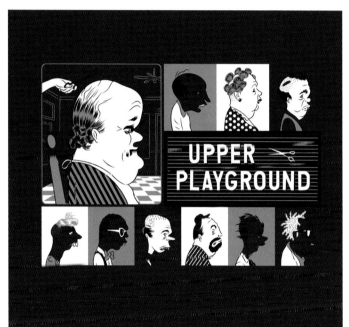

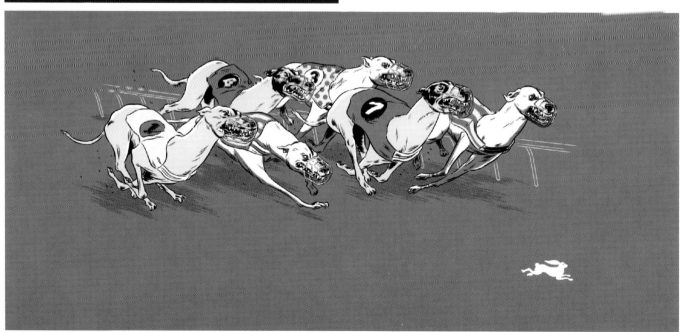

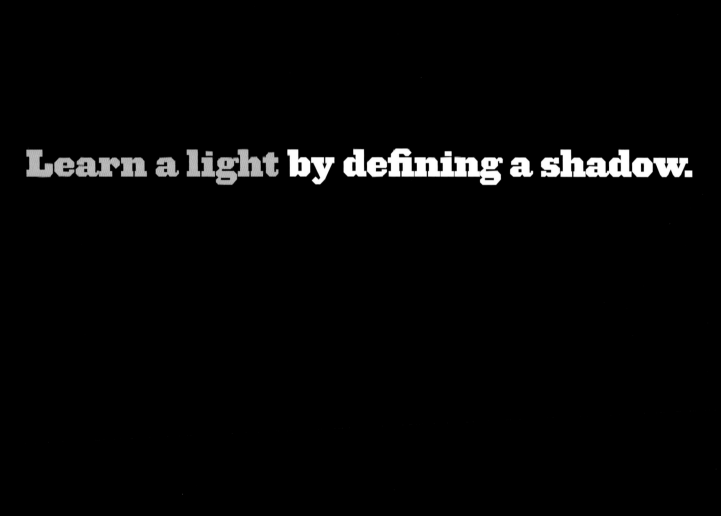

Learn a light by defining a shadow.

USUGROW

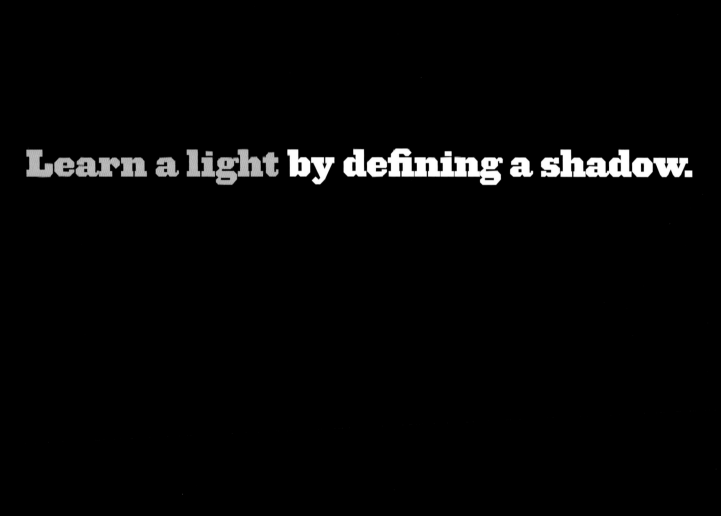

1162
MUNK
ONE

1163
MUNK
ONE

1164
MUNK
ONE

1165
MUNK
ONE

UPPER PLAYGROUND

1173
OBLVN

1174
OBLVN

1175
BEN
TOUR

PLAYGROUND

1177
SABER

1178
SABER

1179
SABER

1180
SABER

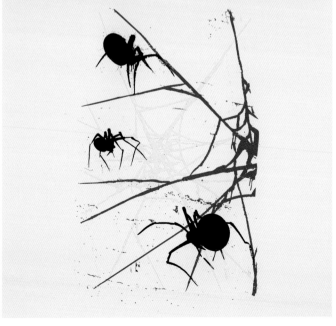

1181
SABER

1182
SABER

1183
SABER

1184
**LUDE
BEHAVIOR**

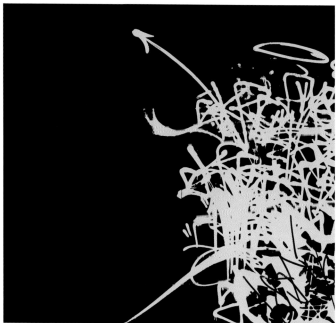

1185
HANNAH STOUFFER

1186
HANNAH STOUFFER

1187
DAVID ELLIS

1188
DAVID ELLIS

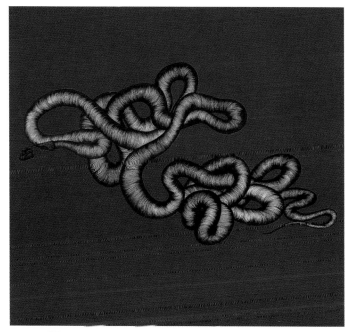

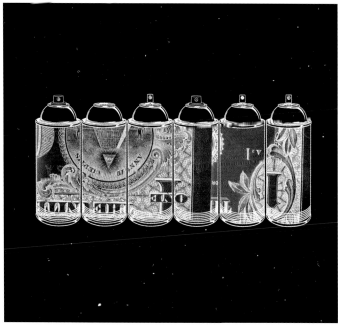

ITS
ALIT
TLES
CARY

UP
PER
PLAY
GR
OUND

1192
PATRICK MARTINEZ

1193
PATRICK MARTINEZ

1194
PATRICK MARTINEZ

UPPER PLAYGROUND

1203
IDEALIST

1204
VISION LAB

1205
MORNING BREATH

1206
CHRIS LEE

1210
MARCO ZAMORA

1211
MARCO ZAMORA

1212
MARCO ZAMORA

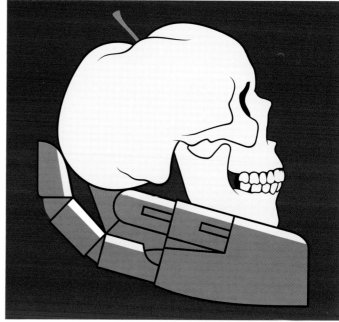

RINZEN RINZEN HYDRO 74 MARIO WAGNER

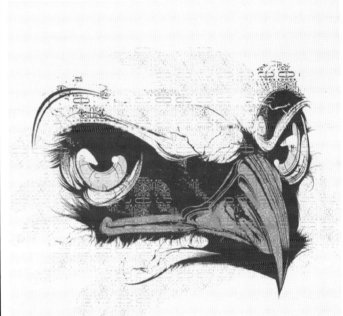

dark side of the bay

TWØ THØUS AND NINE

The late writer David Foster Wallace once said in an interview, "The world that I live in consists of 250 advertisements a day and any number of unbelievably entertaining options, most of which are subsidized by corporations that want to sell me things. The whole way that the world acts on my nerve endings is bound up with stuff that the guys with leather patches on their elbows would consider pop or trivial or ephemeral." In a weird way, Upper Playground has always fit this Wallace mode; a brand of the times, but always ten steps ahead, outside looking in, fighting against a world of preconceived ideas of cool and popularity. Upper Playground has always tried to stay true to creative spirit and collected the energy of the contemporary artists that represent our times. In reality, how does an independent brand survive in a world of big business marketing budgets and mass-produced corporate waste? UP simply just stayed real to the audience they represent. They fed, nurtured, and gained from the art culture with the culture's energy and individualism. It fights off the corporate suit and always presents the vision of the creative mind in a world sometimes devoid of real creativity. That is why it has lasted 10 years and continues into another decade.

As Upper Playground began 09, the FIFTY24SF Gallery in San Francisco was still lively with excitement from monumental exhibits in late 2008 by London's Paul Insect, Barcelona-based Miss Van, and the "Barbary Coast" themed-show from San Franciscan and SuperFishal label head, Jeremy Fish. Fine artist Ron English was setting up shop at FIFTY24SF Gallery for a January exhibition. Seattle, Los Angeles, Portland, Sacramento, and the London stores continued their regional impacts. Re-designs of both Upper Playground's website and web store, along with UP's online magazine, The Citrus Report, pushed the brand's presence on the World Wide Web even further. After one decade, Upper Playground was continuing to push its brand name toward a path of expansion and progression.

How do you party in celebration of a 10-year old apparel and lifestyle brand? For one, you create products that pertain to your anniversary (For Upper Playground, that means this book, special T-shirts, collaborations with other creative companies, gallery shows, perhaps even a real party). But as much as Upper Playground and its founders want to be retrospective, 10 years of the brand is a time to look ahead, to the future, and to the possibilities of being a premier creative lifestyle brand in the next 10 years.

"I look at the first 10 years as just the foundation or framework of where we want to take UP," Mr. Revelli says. "That means increasing video and multi-media projects that we have only started to build recently. That means cut n' sew, outerwear, grander and more elaborate gallery shows, publishing more book titles, continuing to progress the content on The Citrus Report, and more retail stores in culturally relevant cities. We've only just begun."

So there you have it. Ten years of Upper Playground. It's hard to imagine the art and apparel world without the Walrus. For a decade, through clothing, books, gallery shows, documentaries, and personalities that define a generation, Upper Playground has helped play a part in turning the creative lifestyle into an everyday lifestyle. "Who are they?" you might ask yourself about the brand behind the Walrus before realizing that an entire generation of art and culture is at the heart of Upper Playground. It's not one person nor a small group of people; it's the movement.

1224
ESTEVAN ORIOL

1225
ESTEVAN ORIOL

1226
ESTEVAN ORIOL

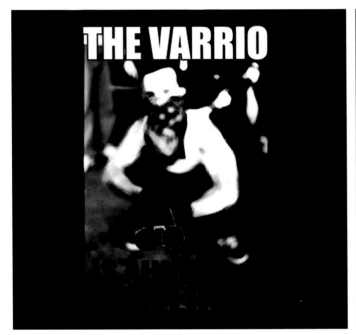

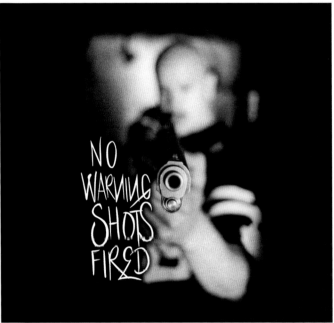

1233
ESTEVAN ORIOL

1234
PATRICK MARTINEZ

1235
PATRICK MARTINEZ

1236

**CALEB
KOZLOWSKI**

1237

**CALEB
KOZLOWSKI**

1238

**CALEB
KOZLOWSKI**

1239
MUNK
ONE

UPPER PLAYGROUND

VS

I enjoy seeing really good artists use their creativity on a tee. When done well, they become works of art. Making tees allows me to create art that is accessible to most people, which makes me feel good. Of course I also like seeing people wearing something with my design on it when I least expect it. I get a kick when someone is still rocking a design I did years ago.

MUNK
ONE

Dope Masters®

1244
MUNK
ONE

1245
MUNK
ONE

1246
MUNK
ONE

DENIS
KENNEDY

DENIS
KENNEDY

DENIS
KENNEDY

DENIS
KENNEDY

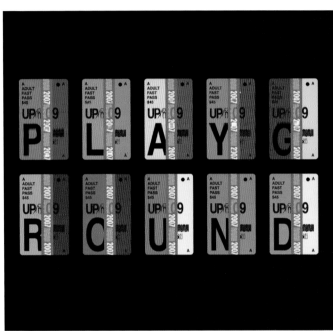

1255
MORNING BREATH

1256
MORNING BREATH

1257
MORNING BREATH

1258
MORNING BREATH

MORNING
BREATH

MORNING
BREATH

MORNING
BREATH

MORNING
BREATH

1263
HERA

1264
HERA

1265
CRAOLA

1266
CRAOLA

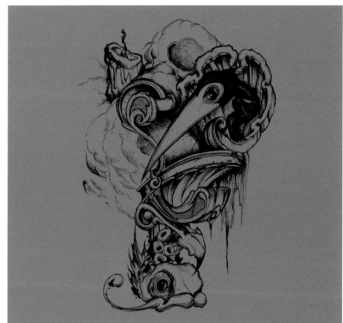

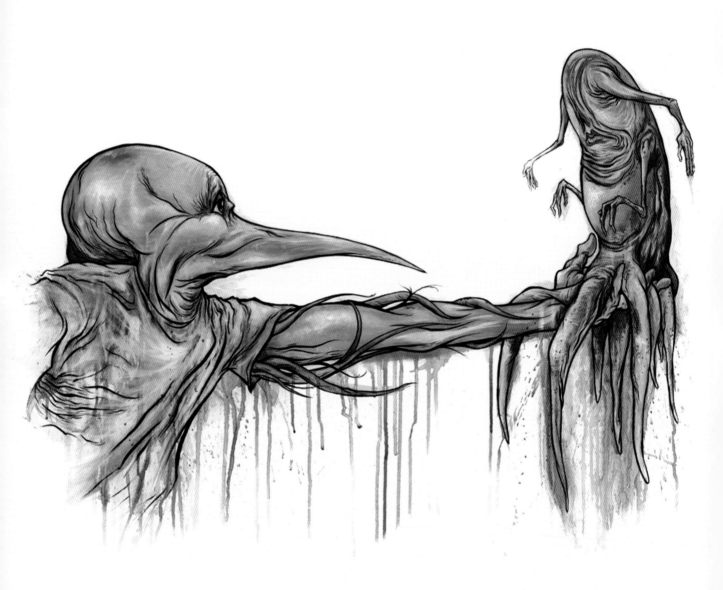

This is my rifle.
There are MANY like it, but this one is mine.

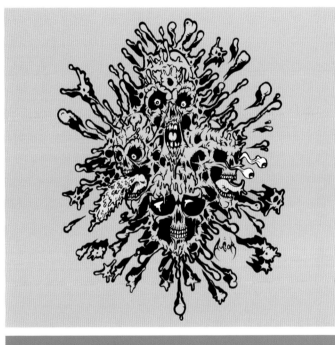

1275
ADNAUSEUM

1276
ADNAUSEUM

1277
ADNAUSEUM

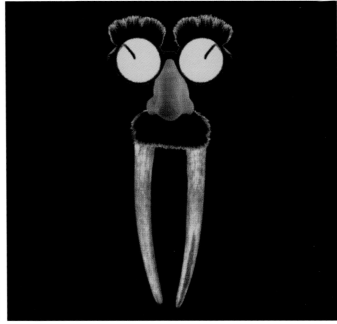

CODY
HUDSON

MAXX 242

EL MAC

KENYON BAJUS

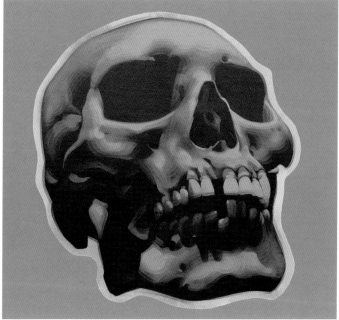

1287
KORALIE

1288
CODY
HUDSON

1289
KORALIE

1290
JEREMY FISH

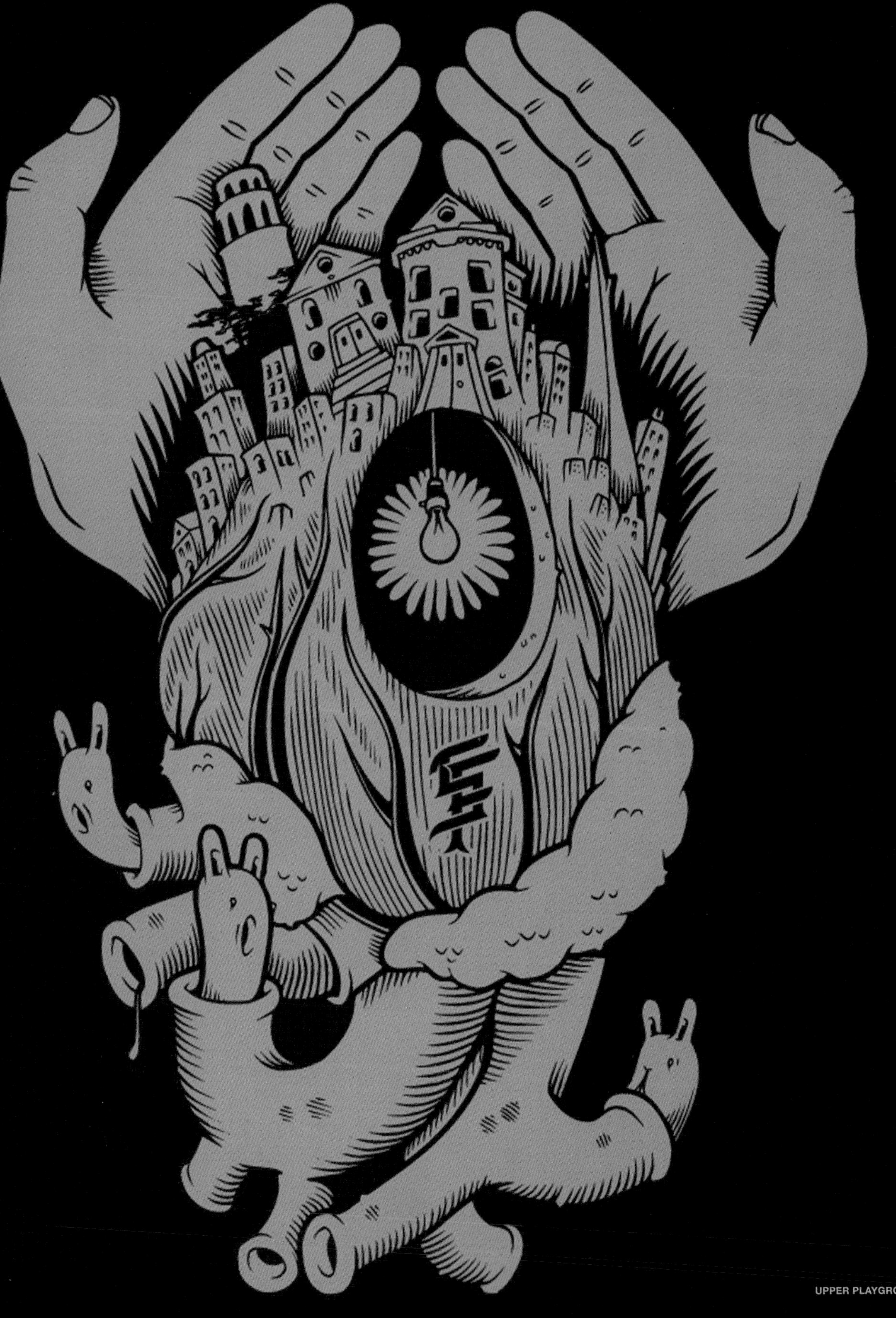

UPPER PLAYGROUND

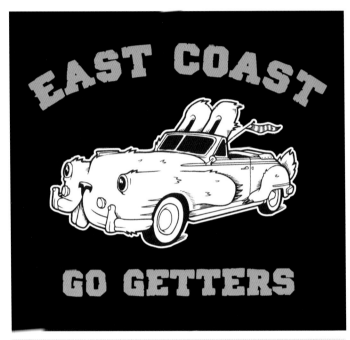

1295
JEREMY FISH

1296
JEREMY FISH

1297
JEREMY FISH

1298
JEREMY FISH

1303
JEREMY FISH

1304
JEREMY FISH

1301
JEREMY FISH

1302
JEREMY FISH

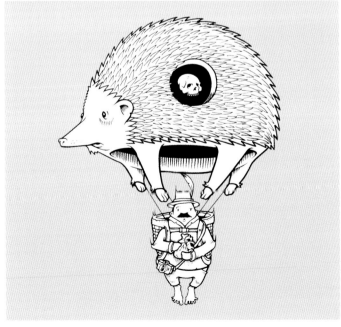

1303
SAM
FLORES

1304
SAM
FLORES

1305
SAM
FLORES

1306
SAM
FLORES

SAM
FLORES

SAM
FLORES

SAM
FLORES

SAM
FLORES

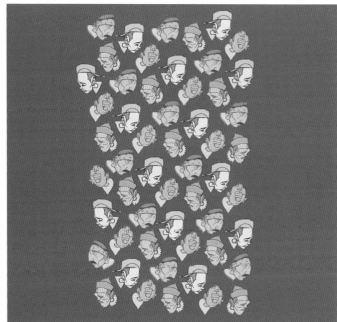

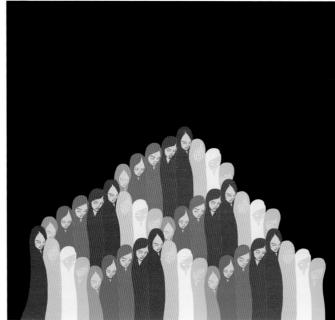

1313
SAM FLORES

1314
SAM FLORES

1315
SAM FLORES

1316
SAM FLORES

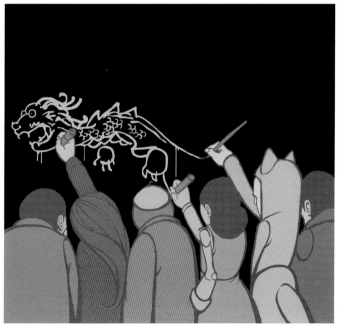

SAM
FLORES

SAM
FLORES

SAM
FLORES

1320
DENIS KENNEDY

1321
DENIS KENNEDY

1322
OBLVN

1323
OBLVN

1327
AARON HORKEY

1328
SAELEE OH

1339
DAVID CHOE

1330
EO

DAN
CUENCA

DIFF'RENT SPOKES

44

FOR
DIFF'RENT
FOLKS

IN THE HEART ØF THE CITY

CITY TEES
MICHAEL LANGAN
DENIS KENNEDY
ADNAUSEUM
DUST LA ROCK
GROTESK
CHUBY
JEREMY FISH
REVOK
JEREMYVILLE
SAM FLORES
BRIAN FLYNN
MUNK ONE
GREG "CRAOLA" SIMKINS
CODY HUDSON
ALEX PARDDD
SUPPOZ

UPPER
PLAYGROUND

DENIS
KENNEDY

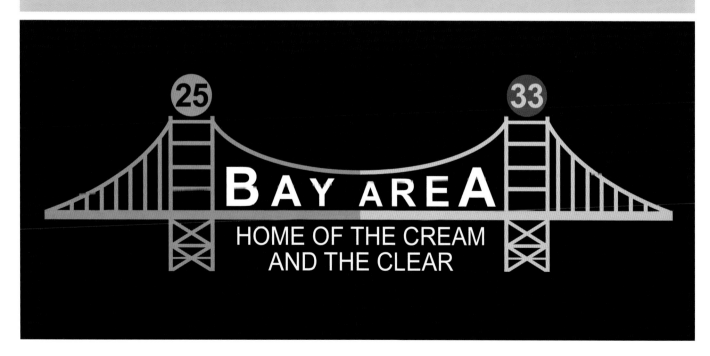

SAN FRANFUCKINGCISCO

25   33

BAY AREA

HOME OF THE CREAM
AND THE CLEAR

1335
DENIS
KENNEDY

1336
DENIS
KENNEDY

1337
DENIS
KENNEDY

1333
DENIS
KENNEDY

DENIS
KENNEDY

DENIS
KENNEDY

DENIS
KENNEDY

DENIS
KENNEDY

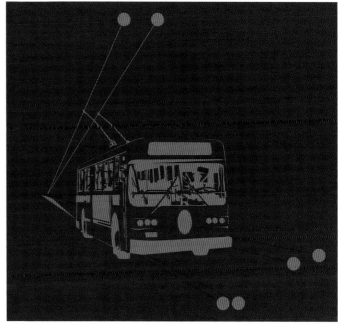

1344
CHUEY

1345
JEREMY
FISH

1346
DENIS
KENNEDY

1347
JEREMY
FISH

DENIS
KENNEDY

BRIAN
FLYNN

DENIS
KENNEDY

UPPER PLAYGROUND
"STRAIGHT OUTTA FRISCO"

SAN FRANCISCO
UPPER PLAYGROUND

1353
CHUEY

1354
CHUEY

1355
CHUEY

1356
CHUEY

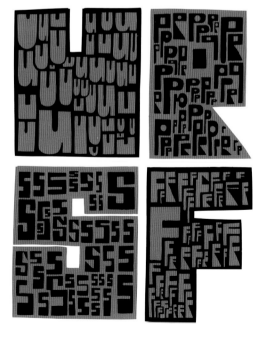

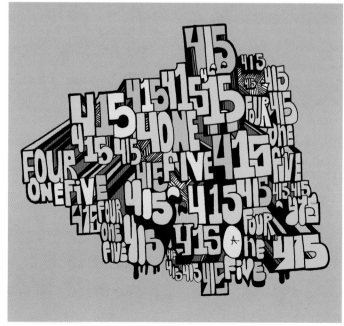

1360
DENIS KENNEDY

1361
DENIS KENNEDY

1362
DENIS KENNEDY

1363
SAM FLORES

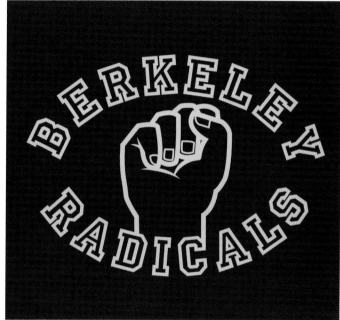

OAKLAND

1365
**DENIS
KENNEDY**

1366
**DENIS
KENNEDY**

1367
**DENIS
KENNEDY**

**DENIS
KENNEDY**

**DENIS
KENNEDY**

**BRIAN
FLYNN**

1371
DENIS KENNEDY

1372
BRIAN FLYNN

1373
DENIS KENNEDY

The Freshmaker

ATTACK of THE BIG TOMATO

UPPER PLAYGROUND
SACRAMENTO, CA.

1376
DENIS KENNEDY

1377
MUNK ONE

1378
CRAOLA

1379
DENIS KENNEDY

ONE NIGHT IN TOKYO

AS TOLD BY SAM FLORES

During the last seven years working with Upper Playground, I've got to travel all over the world. My first trip was to Japan many years ago, when I went with Bigfoot, Mike Giant, and Matt from UP.

I remember the last night there that the hosts wanted to take us out for a nice, traditional Japanese dinner. It was one of those personal rooms with the chairs surrounding a huge table with a long, rectangular surface in the middle where they cook the food right in front of you. We all ordered okonomiyaki, which is a traditional Japanese omelet, like a huge egg pancake filled with shredded lettuce, potato, and cheese. They're great, so the evening started as normal as it can when dining with a Giant, a Bigfoot, and me!

The pints of beer were flowing, everyone was enjoying themselves, with the hosts at one end of the long table mostly just watching, smiling, and nodding, ordering us beer after beer. Across from me is Giant and Biggie, and they were more in their own little conversation, leaning in to each other whispering things, looking at their glasses laughing and giggling.

Maybe I should have mentioned this at the beginning, but this happened to be the last day you could legally buy mushrooms on the streets in Tokyo. I found this strange that you were able to buy something like that in such a strict and no joke city such as Tokyo. Giant had found a small stand not far from the restaurant and purchased a bag of those shriveled-up buggers. Having little trouble at all convincing Bigfoot to partake in the festivities, especially being that the mushrooms were from the same place the Sasquatch himself was from (nature!), I myself had to pass, on the grounds that I'm done with that shit. I wanted to keep some tiny semblance of composure at dinner with our grateful hosts and I'm done with that shit!

Cut back to dinner, and I keep looking over at our babbling brothers, their faces starting to get red, laughing, and bursting of giggles and chuckles. Then Giant leans over at Biggie and whispers something into his right ear, and suddenly Big's eyes go huge while staring straight into his empty pint glass. Big jumps up from his seat knocking his chair backwards, stands at the far end of our table holding his glass with both hands staring into it while giving off this low-pitched, high volume moan. I don't know if any of you have met Bigfoot or heard him talk, but he sounds like a mix between Bobcat Goldthwait and Charles Manson if he were from Jersey. "What's wrong, man?" I ask, watching him start to rock back and forth like Rainman when smoke alarms go off. "AAAAHHHHNNNH MAAAN, THERRRE'S AN IIIINDIIAAN HEEAD INNN THHHHE BOTTOM OF MMMMYYYY BEEEERRR, IIIIMMMM SORRRYYY!!," he sort of screams quietly.

I said to him, "Why are you sorry Bigfoot, it's cool!" I was trying to assure him. "NOOOO MANNN, IIIMMMM SOOORRRYY FOR ALL THE WHIIIITE MAAAANNN steeealing yourrr laaannnd mann!!," Big said. He was loud and quiet like that.

Now the whole restaurant is quiet and everyone is staring at him. The waiter had just walked in and his jaw has dropped too, carrying a fresh tray of beers that were going to the guy whining in the corner! Bigfoot then starts to cry, causing Giant to stand up, having not a strong reaction to the mushrooms, and realizes its time to get the sad Bigfoot back to the table. He tells him everything is going to be okay, just sit

back down, and says "See the nice man has brought you a new beer, look!" "NNNOOOO MAANN, THE INDIIIAAN," Bigfoot says. "Nope, there is NOO more Indian, see!" Giant says quickly, and grabs his pint glass and shakes it, suds flying, destroying the invisible Indian head.

Bigfoot freaks out and says he has to get out of there, storms out and jumps into an elevator. I start laughing because as Biggie was walking out, he gave us all one last look back, and it looked just like that famous photo of the Bigfoot in the forest looking over his shoulder. After he left everyone had a little laugh, and looking at the hosts, they couldn't have been happier. They never get to see anything like that; that was their first Bigfoot sighting. They loved the dinner, and even though I thought they would be shocked and embarrassed, they felt the exact opposite. After a few minutes, Giant decided to go downstairs to check up on our Sasquatch friend.

We all drank and finished our okonomiyaki, then I realized it had been about a half-hour and we just let the two weirdest characters in Tokyo loose on the town high on 'shrooms! I take the elevator down to see if

I can locate my peoples, when I see across the street a huge crowd gathering around. I ran over, pushed my way past the people and camera flashes, where there stands a crazed Bigfoot drawing this huge crazy mural with a big magnum black marker humming a Kiss song to himself. Giant is laughing to himself on the side taking photos of the crowd taking photos. I looked to my left and there was a line of Japanese police walking towards us. See during this trip, the World Cup was being held in Japan, so the security was beefed up with swat teams everywhere. I figured this was a fine time to get these beserkers out of dodge, and I scurried the two of them off down the street to a bar called Gas Panic.

The whole day prior to dinner, Biggie had been going on and on about meeting and hooking up with a girl. At this point a few of us in our party started making jokes as we stumbled down the stairs to Gas Panic. We started putting up bets if Bigfoot would hook up with a girl, or if he could even meet one at this point. We all did a few shots of this fluorescent green hangover liquid and then realized we lost Bigfoot again. After carefully scanning the bar,

we see, in a dark corner, Biggie talking to the hottest girl I've seen all night. He wasn't just talking to her; she was smiling, laughing, and flirting back. She was wearing his sunglasses, and I think a Bigfoot sticker was now on one of her breasts. Well shit! We all made one of those, "OOOOOOOOOOEEEE!!" noises, like if you got to see Jordan make a winning shot at the buzzer. Everyone started changing their bets, started added more money, saying, "Oh it's totally fucking on!"

Most of us go outside to have a celebratory cigarette. A few minutes later, up walks Bigfoot by himself. We're all standing there, asking, "What happened man?" He just looked at us and said, "AAAHHHHHHHNNH MAAAAN, I ASKED HER WHAT TYPE OF MUSIC SHE LIKEEES MAAAN, AND SHE SAIIIIDDD LINKIN PARKK. ITS ALLL ABOOOUT AC/DC!!" And then he walked away into the night, as we stood there, dumbfounded, looking at each other.

Portland

1386
BRIAN
FLYNN

1387
BRIAN
FLYNN

1388
BRIAN
FLYNN

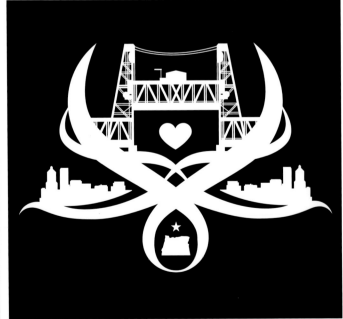

1393

DENIS
KENNEDY

1394

BRIAN
FLYNN

1395

SUPPOZ

1396
DENIS
KENNEDY

1397
DENIS
KENNEDY

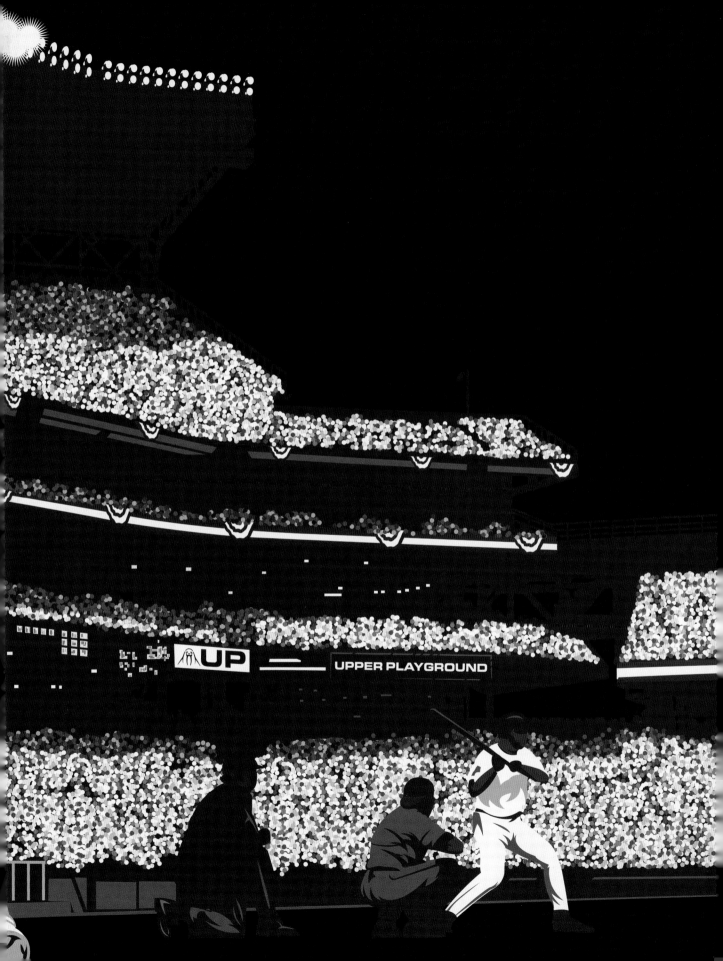

1399
JEREMY
FISH

1400
JEREMY
FISH

AN AMERICAN WALRUS IN LONDON

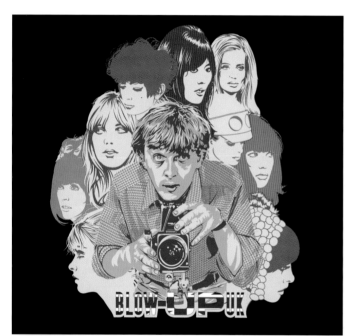